Easy Blackjack
For the
Average Joe

EASY
BLACKJACK
For The

AVERAGE JOE

By Billy Joe Garner

ISBN: 0-9763405-0-X

Acknowledgements

I would like to thank Kathy Panogas, Dr. Jeffrey Steele, Dr. David Yingling, and my brother, Larry Garner for all of their help in editing out my many mistakes. I would also like to thank Brad Davis for his excellent photography.

If you think you might have a gambling problem, contact Gamblers Anonymous at:
P. O. Box 17173
Los Angeles, CA 90017
(213) 386-8789
www.gamblersanonymous.org/

Contact Information
On the web at averagejoeblackjack.com
Email at avgjoe@charter.net

Table of Contents

Introduction / 1

Chapter One
  How Blackjack Is Played / 7

Chapter Two
  Basic Strategy for the Average Joe / 17
    Thorp Basic Strategy / 18
    E-Z Basic Strategy / 20

Chapter Three
  How To Learn Basic Strategy / 25
    Hard Standing and Hitting / 25
    Hard Doubling Down / 27
    Soft Doubling Down/Soft Hands / 27
    Pairs / 29
    Difficult to Learn Hands / 30

Chapter Four
  Problem Hands and Dilemmas / 33
    Problem Hands 1-7 / 34-40
    Surrender / 41
    Insurance / 42

Chapter Five
  Progressive Betting Systems / 45
    The Martingale / 46
    Simple Systems / 47
    Intermediate Systems / 50
    Advanced Systems / 55
    Proportional Betting / 57

Chapter Six
    Betting for the Average Joe / 59

Chapter Seven
    Joe, Do The Math / 71

Chapter Eight
    If You Must Count / 87

Chapter Nine
    Money Management / 93
        Bankroll / 95
        Chips / 95
        Win and Loss Limits / 96
        Discipline / 98
        Mr. Black / 99
        Mrs. Green / 101

Chapter Ten
    Advice for Picking a Table / 103
    Things to Remember / 105
    Making E-Z Bet Work For You / 106

Glossary / 110

Index / 117

References / 120

About the Author / 122

Introduction

The casino is your enemy. Don't ever forget that.

Casinos are some of the most spectacular places on earth. They were built with the money of losers. Every game they offer has a built in *take*, or profit. Some are higher than others, but they all favor the casino.

A casino is like the Venus flytrap. You may recall from biology class how the flytrap attracts the unsuspecting insect into the trap. Once there, the trap closes around them and they can't escape. The casino is an attractive place, both inside and out. It has a lure that is hard to resist- the lure of money. You can win money. You can get lucky, and you can become rich. You can eat, drink and be merry. So the casino offers cheap food, free drinks, great shows, waitresses with low cut...enough of that. You get the point - the casino is the flytrap and you are the fly.

Casinos invented their games and did so with a calculated take. There is a game that they didn't invent. It was originally known as *vingt-et-un,* or twenty-one. This was the predecessor of the modern game of Blackjack. Had the casinos invented the game, I can assure you it would have a higher take. It would be unbeatable. But, they didn't and it is not.

Casinos have a high profit margin on every game they offer. They have high profits from Blackjack because it is a very popular game and so many players do not even know basic strategy. However, a perfectly played basic strategy can get the casino take down to about 0.5% to 0.6%. Find a single deck game and you can get it down to 0.168%. This is about as good as it gets. So how can you get the odds in your favor?

Two techniques have evolved to give the player an edge over the casino. The first technique is card counting. Card counting was conceived back in the 1960s and for a while was very profitable. The player doesn't actually "count" cards and a photographic memory is not needed. Generally, a counter assigns a plus one value to the small cards and a minus one to the larger cards. The player then keeps a running count as the cards are played. As small cards are depleted and large ones are concentrated in the remaining decks, the player has an advantage. One simply bets more during the favorable periods and less during the unfavorable periods.

The second technique is to vary ones bet with the hope of winning more than if flat betting. Many systems have been invented, ranging from simple to very complex. This book introduces many of these progressive systems including two that developed from my research. I hope to give you a slight edge at the Blackjack table and help you win some money. Some of you would be satisfied with just breaking even. I think we can handle that easily. I am not going to make grandiose promises of riches beyond your wildest dreams. I am not going to tell you that you'll win 79% of the time. I am not going to make you into a hotshot professional gambler.

What I want to do is give you - the occasional Blackjack player, the amateur who goes to Vegas once a year, or who takes an occasional weekend to Atlantic City, *the average Joe* - some sound advice and techniques you can learn with a few hours of study and practice. Mastering a counting system would take months of practice. Would you practice months to play a little better on your annual vacation? You can learn a progressive betting sequence in a matter of minutes. It may take a couple of hours to learn a basic strategy. This (plus a little common sense about money management) can go a long way at the tables.

If you are reading this book for a new and improved counting system, you've got the wrong book. I have included a ten-tracking system to help you with playing decisions. This is not as precise as real plus-minus systems. It is "ballpark" information. Most decisions in Blackjack are easy if you know the basic strategy. Still other decisions are much easier if you know whether the ten count favors the player or the dealer. In that respect, tracking tens can be useful to the non-counter.

If you are reading this book because you want to learn about betting progressions, you have the right book. I have compiled a group of progression sequences and I have developed a few also. I have also developed a tool to evaluate a betting sequence before you have money on the table. There are wide ranging profits among the listed sequences. This tool allows the reader to put a sequence side by side with others and see what the differences are. I give full credit to the author and may make comments regarding the book from which it was obtained.

In this book you will find a new basic strategy developed for Blackjack that was tested by simulating over one trillion hands (that's right - *trillion*). Inside you will find two new winning progressions developed from my research. They have been both mathematically and casino tested. Also inside you are going to find two negative progression sequences that lose *less* than flat betting. And finally, you are going to find some advice about insuring Blackjacks, doubling on an eleven, and other problem hands that come up.

I am not a professional gambler and don't want to be. I make a good living and enjoy what I do. I just want to play a game that I love, beat a multi-million dollar casino and not have to concentrate non-stop through a six-deck shoe. I don't want a 1% advantage - I want a 5% advantage. I want to have fun playing Blackjack and not lose my shirt. I am the average Joe.

Blackjack has been around American gaming halls since the turn of the 20th century, but has only been scientifically studied since the 1950s. In 1953, Baldwin, Cantey, Maisel and McDermott began a study that was published in 1956 entitled "The Optimum Strategy in Blackjack." Early in the 1960's an IBM computer expert, Julian Braun, ran some nine billion hands of blackjack on his computer and developed the statistics for what became the first basic strategy. In 1962, Dr. Edward O. Thorp published a book on Blackjack, *Beat The Dealer*, [1] and the popularity of Blackjack soared. Since then hundreds of books have been written on the game and modifications to the basic strategy have been made, but the core is still intact.

In this book you will find a basic strategy that evolved from the Thorp Basic Strategy and others. Thorp's strategy was designed for single deck Blackjack, but single deck is hard to find outside of Nevada or Mississippi. Often a six-deck game is offered. The basic strategy that I designed, E-Z Basic Strategy, was originally for six-deck Blackjack. Once in its final form, I ran billions more studies to see how it performed against four, two and single deck Blackjack. To my surprise, it performed very well. The biggest surprise was when I decided to test it against Dr. Thorp's single deck strategy. I ran 150 billion hands with E-Z Basic Strategy and compared it to 51 billion using the Thorp strategy. E-Z Basic Strategy came out on top. I feel very confident E-Z Basic Strategy is the only basic strategy you need to learn. It probably wasn't necessary to run over a trillion hands, but it gives me confidence in the validity of my numbers. The strategy is a little different from others, so, if you have learned another strategy, you will see some minor changes.

Most of the early authors (and some current ones) emphasized a card counting system derived from and similar to the first card counting system invented by Dr. Thorp. Very little advice was given to the casual, weekend gambler except to follow the basic strategy. Everyone agreed that the Martingale system of doubling your bets after losing was too risky, but no alternatives were offered.

According to Dr. Thorp, "No betting scheme can ever be devised that will have the slightest effect upon the casino's long-run advantage". So the reader was led to believe that only by counting cards could one win. Unfortunately, casinos do not like card counting, and, if suspected of counting, the player could be barred from ever playing there again. Furthermore, to master a counting system took a tremendous amount of practice. Casino countermeasures such as multiple decks were instituted to minimize the effect of counters. The average Joe was either unable to master a counting system, or didn't have the time to put in just to play a little Blackjack.

My search for an alternative to counting cards led me to do a literature search, and I found a number of progressive betting systems. A chapter is devoted to the most promising systems found. In the next chapter you are taken step-by-step through the process of developing E-Z Bet. Some of my computer simulation data aided in its development.

I also developed a simple but effective tool to evaluate most progressive betting systems. Another chapter is devoted to simply "doing the math" to allow you to compare the systems. You will be able to see what makes a winning system. The results are consolidated in a table so you can easily compare them. Also included is the best advice regarding proper bankroll, discipline, managing your money, and miscellaneous advice. This will be found in Chapter Nine. The best system in the world would not make a winner of you without proper money management. For now, let's start off with the basics of how to play Blackjack.

How Blackjack Is Played

Dealer's Side

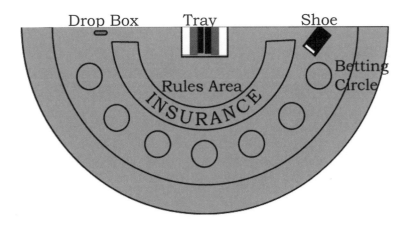

Players' Side

The Blackjack Table

The designations in the diagram are explained in the following text.

This chapter is written for the novice Blackjack player. It is an overview designed to get the novice started playing. Rules vary from casino to casino so some of the options to play are not always available. Be sure you ask about the rules before playing. If you need clarification, ask the dealer or supervisor, also known as the *pit boss*.

The object of Blackjack, or 21, is to win by either exceeding the card count of the dealer or to win by the dealer busting. Blackjack is played using one to eight decks of 52 cards. Single and two deck Blackjack is dealt by hand, and generally face down. Four, six or eight-deck Blackjack is dealt from a box, or *shoe*, one card at a time and face up. Cards can be shuffled in different ways. Single deck and two deck blackjack is traditionally shuffled by the dealer. Multiple decks may also be shuffled by the dealer, or may be shuffled by shuffling machines. Relatively new to the scene are continuous-shuffling machines, or C.S.M. With a C.S.M., after each hand or two the dealer places the played cards into the back of the machine where they are mixed with the rest of the cards and replayed.

Cards are valued according to their number. The suit of the card is irrelevant in the standard game of Blackjack. Cards numbered 2 through 10 have a value of their number. Face cards have a value of 10, and the Ace has a dual value of 1 or 11. For instance, a 9-5 hand has a total of 9 + 5 or 14. An Ace-5 would total 6 if the Ace were counted as 1, or 16 when counted as 11.

You may hold your two cards when face down, but should not even touch them when they are face up. You should not verbally tell the dealer your wishes because should there be a conflict, the cameras, or *eye in the sky*, would not pick up your voice. Signals are used to communicate your wishes to the dealer. With the cards in hand, use them to scratch the surface of the table in front of your bet to signal you would like to *hit* (take a card), or gently place them face down under your *wager, or bet,* to indicate you wish to *stand* (take no more cards). In face up Blackjack you must point to your cards or tap the table behind them to hit, and to stand you must wave your hand gently with the palm toward the dealer. Place an extra bet out and indicate to the dealer if you want to double down or split your cards. Surrender should be said to the dealer, or signaled by drawing an imaginary line with your finger in front of the betting circle.

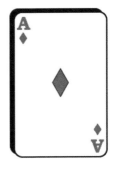 

A *Blackjack* (a.k.a. a Natural) is any Ace-ten combination and is obviously the best hand you can be dealt. When the player is dealt Blackjack, the payoff is one and one half times the wager (3:2) unless the dealer also has Blackjack. If both the dealer and player have Blackjack, this is a *push,* or tie. You may encounter games where a blackjack is paid less than 3:2. This may have been changed to offer a single deck game in an era of a scarcity of single deck games. Other less profitable options may have been added such as surrender to compensate the player for the loss of the blackjack premium.

When the dealer's up card is an Ace, play is paused for a side bet called insurance. *Insurance* is a side bet on whether the dealer has a ten-value card in the hole. The odds favor the casino so most authors advise against taking insurance at any time. An insurance bet is one half of the bet you currently have out, and is placed in front of your betting circle on the area marked INSURANCE (see illustration). Insurance is paid two to one, so the side bet you placed will pay double if the dealer does in fact have Blackjack. The dealer will then peek at the hole card next to see if he/she has a ten card in the hole. If the dealer doesn't have Blackjack, the side bet is taken away and play resumes.

Some authors advise insuring your Blackjack against a dealer Ace. Their reasoning is that you will win at least even money if he has it or doesn't. If you don't insure a Blackjack and push, then you will have gained nothing for the best possible hand. Recall the old adage "a little of something is better than all of nothing." This is a rational argument, but it will be your call. Just remember the odds are against it and you should be consistent when taking insurance. Don't insure your Blackjack one time and not the next. You might guess wrong. A more thorough discussion will follow in Chapter Four.

Each table has a minimum and maximum bet limit. To play, you must purchase chips. Chips are used in place of money. Each denomination of chip is a different color. Place your money on the table in front of you and ask for the denomination of chips you want. Red chips are $5 denomination; green chips are worth $25; black chips are worth $100. Do not place your money in the *betting circle* (see small circles on illustration) or the dealer may assume you are betting the whole amount on the next hand. Once dealt, there is no backing out, so be careful. The dealer will inspect your money and give you a stack of chips. Count them and put them in stacks of five in front of you. Then place your first bet in the betting circle. Never touch the chips after the deal begins - the house might think you are cheating.

The dealer will deal from his/her left to right going around twice to give everyone two cards. The dealer will start to his/her left (*first base*) and proceed to the right, settling with each player until they reach the last position, which is called *third base*. Once all of the players have made their stands, busted, or been paid for their Blackjacks, the dealer exposes the hole card and concludes the hand. The dealer then picks up the cards and lost bets, or pays the winners and picks up their cards.

The player has several options when his/her time to play arrives. If you have a good hand or a *pat* hand and wish not to take additional cards, signal to stand. A *pat hand* is a hand with a value between 17 and 21. If you need another card, signal for a hit (also called *draw*). You may hit until you are ready to stand, or you *bust*. To bust, or *break,* is to exceed a count of 21. You lose if you bust, or the dealer's card count exceeds yours without his/her busting. Your cards and bet are immediately taken away when you bust.

You may stop at any point up to 21, but the dealer must exceed 16. Most casinos require the dealer to hit an Ace-6, also called a soft 17, while others require the dealer to stand on a soft 17. If you beat the dealer's total or the dealer busts, you are paid an amount equal to your *bet* or *wager.* If your hand is less than the dealer's or you bust, you lose your wager. If your hand ties (pushes) the dealer, no chips change hands. The player has to make his/her decision first. This gives an edge to the casino.

Hard Hands

The hand of 9-5 above is an example of a *hard hand.*

A hard hand is a hand that has a firm value. Other examples are 6-5, Queen-7, 2-10, or 3-5. The 6-5 hand has a value of 11. Eleven is a great hand with which to double down. The Queen is valued as a ten, so the Queen-7 has a value of 17. This is an example of a pat hand. The 2-10 hand has a value of 12. This is a *stiff hand*. A stiff hand is one which may bust if hit. The 3-5 totals only 8 so this hand can be hit with any card safely and not bust.

Soft Hands

The Ace-4 is an example of a *soft hand*. A soft hand is a hand that includes an Ace when the Ace is counted as an 11. Because the Ace has dual values, a soft hand also has dual values. The Ace-4 has a value of 15, but also has a value of 5. So when the Ace is counted as 11, the hand is still soft, but when it must be counted as 1 to prevent busting, it becomes a hard hand.

Soft hands can always be hit and not bust due to the Ace being counted as eleven. However, you may not want to hit some soft hands. An example is a soft 20 (Ace-9). Soft hands may also be doubled down on. As with lower value hard hands, lower value soft hands may be improved by hitting them. Hitting also may worsen them. Hit a soft 17 and draw a five through nine, and your situation is worsened. The Basic Strategy, found on page 23 in the following chapter, guides your play. It tells you the mathematically correct move to make for each hand you are dealt.

Doubling Down

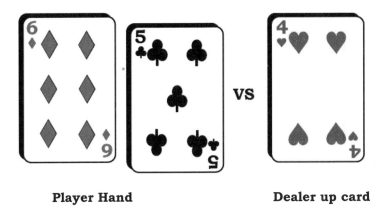

Player Hand   **Dealer up card**

Another option you may have is to *double down* or, commonly, just *double*. When doubling down, you are allowed to place an additional bet equal to your current bet and double the wager. What you give up is the option to receive more than one card. Certain situations have a good chance of success and the doubling option is your best bet. The 11 versus the dealer's four above is an example of an excellent double down situation. The rules range from doubling on any two cards to doubling on ten and eleven only.

Doubling down increases your risk, so it should be given extra thought; however, it can also be very profitable, so don't be overly cautious. The best double down hands are noted in the Basic Strategy. Keep in mind that it is an option and, with a large bet out, one may wish to simply hit and not risk extra losses. This would allow you to take more than one card, if needed.

Of special note is when you have a pair of fives. Pairs can be *split* into two hands (see next section). Tell the dealer you are doubling down and not splitting the two fives. To split would not be the right move, but the dealer could misunderstand your wishes.

Pairs

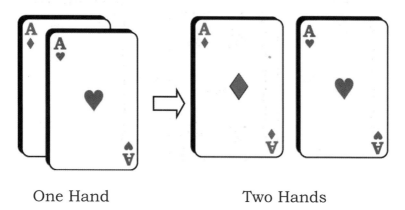

One Hand   Two Hands

Pairs of like cards can be *split* into two hands with an additional wager equal to the original one. To split a pair, lay them down (if holding them), and place a second bet on one of the cards. If you are playing face up, tell the dealer and place the second bet out. Do not touch the cards. Each of the cards then becomes the basis for an individual hand that may be hit until you stand or bust. Once the first hand is completed, signal to the dealer to move to the second hand and hit it until you complete it. The <u>exception</u> is the example above. Once Aces are split you only get one card on each Ace.

You may be able to double down on a hand after splitting, which would require a third bet. Also, you may receive another of the same value cards and be able to re-split the new pair. Refer to the Basic Strategy in the next chapter to learn which pairs should be split, and when to do it in relation to the dealer up card.

A stiff hand is a hand with a value of 12 through 16. These are hands that can bust if hit - and you will get a lot of them. Many of your hardest decisions will be when dealt a stiff hand. A pat hand has a hard value of 17 through 21. These are <u>never</u> hit. You stand and hope for the best.

When the dealer potentially has a stiff hand (2-6 up), your choices are made easier. In this case, even if you don't have a pat hand, you will stand at less than 17. Your hope is that the dealer will bust. (See the Basic Strategy.) When he/she has a pat hand (presumably), the decisions are harder. I say *presumably* because your assumption is that the dealer has a ten as the hole card and all of your decisions are based on this assumption. The reason for this assumption is that four of the thirteen cards in a suite are ten-value cards so the probability the hole card is a ten-value card is high. Ten-cards actually make up less than 31% of the deck so the assumption of a ten hole card is wrong 69% of the time. The average card value is about 9 (if you count the Ace as 11) so there is just less than a 50% chance the hole card is a 9 or better.

Dealer Bust Rate

The following is a listing of dealer bust rate for each up card. They were derived from the average of four sources.

Dealer Up	2	3	4	5	6	7	8	9	10	A
Bust %	35	38	40	42	42	26	24	23	21	12

These numbers are important because they indicate how vulnerable you are. When you have a stiff hand, and the dealer has a 10 up, you only have a one in five chance if you don't draw to it. A review of this table reinforces why Basic Strategy should be followed strictly. It also shows how vulnerable you are when you double down.

You must do it cautiously when big bets are out, because the dealer always has a greater than 50% chance of totaling 17 or better.

What are you hoping to achieve? You want to get a card total of 19 or better to win. One advantage of having Blackjack simulation software is I can prove what I read or hear. One page the program prints out is win rate per hour for each hand dealt. This printout gives a clear indication of which hands are winners and which are losers. The win rate per hour is dependent on frequency of occurrence but I want to show you the win rate for 16 thru 20 to show you why you want to try to draw to a 19 or better. The following table is an hourly win rate against all dealer up cards, based on a $5 flat bet.

Your Total	Win Rate/Hr.
16	-$12.21
17	-$8.76
18	-$0.49
19	$6.10
2-10s	$26.93

As you can see, 18 is about the break even point. With 19 or above, you are a winner. The program doesn't print out a win rate for just 20, but as you can see, 2-tens do very well. When adjusted for frequency of occurrence, 20 would be about $13.46. This is why your desire is to have a hand value of 19 or better.

Basic Strategy
For the Average Joe

Basic Strategy is the guide for playing Blackjack. It is the foundation of proper play. You would be amazed at how many people will play Blackjack without a thorough knowledge of the fundamentals. I have sat at tables with players betting five or ten times my bet and they only knew a few of the proper moves. One elderly gentleman congratulated me for such good hits when I was simply following basic strategy. While I was gradually gaining chips, he was rapidly losing them.

You see, Blackjack is the sum total of a lot of small percentages. Each wrong move adds to the losing percentage while each correct move adds to the winning percentages. At the end of the day, the mistakes can add up to sizeable losses. Of course, some wrong moves are more disastrous than others. Consistently making the wrong decision with a 12-value hand that occurs with a frequency of 8.31% would be more devastating than the wrong choice with a soft 16, which only occurs at a rate of 1.187%.

The Thorp Basic Strategy

The first Basic Strategy I followed was the first one most players follow: the Thorp Basic Strategy. This has been the Bible of Blackjack, the Ten Eight Commandments of Twenty One, passed down from God to Dr. Thorp from the top of Mount Rose [the mountain that

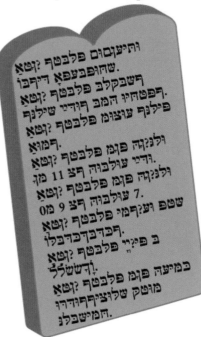

overlooks Reno and Tahoe]. It has been the Gold Standard for playing single deck Blackjack since 1962 and is the basis for all basic strategies that have followed. What has been happening is that these strategies have incorporated minor changes (primarily in the doubling down strategy) leaving the Thorp strategy 90% unchanged. Some authors will print a basic strategy and change just a few plays, essentially plagiarizing Dr. Thorp's Basic Strategy.

This is a copy of the original tablet given to Dr. Thorp by God. The original tablets are kept in a vault in the Luxor Casino. If you can't read Hebrew or you're a little rusty, I have translated it for you on the following page.

Up until the 1980s most play was single deck and most of the basic strategies were for single deck Blackjack. Over time, casinos have changed to multiple decks. This has necessitated slight changes in basic strategy.

Rules have changed as well. Fortunately, modern computer software allows one to develop a basic strategy for the game we play today. I can simply put in the rules that I commonly play under and quickly run billions of hands under different basic strategies. For instance, if I want to look at the benefit of splitting Aces versus a dealer 10 up card, I run two simulations, one with and one without splitting Aces. I then compare the results with this one change and I have an objective analysis.

Thou shalt memorize Basic Strategy.
Thou shalt always split Aces and Eights.
Thou shalt never split Tens.
Thou shalt not double on 11 vs dealer Ace.
Thou shalt not double on 9 vs dealer 7.
Thou shalt insure thy Blackjacks.
Thou shalt quit a WINNER.
Thou shalt not drink excessively when playing.

The way you read the basic strategy table (pg. 23) is to look first to the left side of the strategy. This is the total value of your cards. For instance, a ten and a two would total up to be twelve. Look down the left side of the strategy until you see twelve. To the right of the twelve are the proper moves to make for each of the dealer up-cards. For instance when the dealer has an up card of six, you would stand. If the dealer has a nine up, you would hit your twelve. The legend for each letter is S for stand, H for hit, D for double down, and SP for split.

The Thorp Basic Strategy was the product of nine billion hands played by computers, hence the data gathered should be accurate and the suggested move would be correct in the long run. This strategy was designed to play single deck Blackjack under a specific set of rules. There are thirteen differences between the Thorp Basic Strategy and the strategy in this book, E-Z Basic Strategy. This strategy was developed originally for six-deck Blackjack using state of the art software. For eight-deck strategy, I refer you to David Popik's *Winning Blackjack Without Counting Cards.*[3] In Chapter Five of this book, I will show his betting progression along with other examples.

In 1983 John Patrick wrote *So You Want To Be A Gambler- Blackjack*[4] and introduced a more conservative single deck basic strategy. The reasons for the adjustments are very well explained and primarily deal with doubling down against stronger dealer up cards. The differences are explained by Patrick's respect for dealer 9, 10, and Ace up cards and the dealer's vulnerability with 2-6 up cards. Patrick doubles down with an eight against a dealer 5 or 6 up card. When holding a ten, Patrick doubles only against a dealer's 7 or less. With an 11, he doubles on 8 or less. Also different about Patrick's Basic Strategy is his splitting of Aces. He doesn't split always. He splits Aces against 8 or less. This is a more conservative approach to Blackjack. I highly recommend you read his book.

Development of E-Z Basic Strategy

Thorp and Patrick represent the two extremes of basic strategy. Many others lie between the two. Some prefer a conservative strategy when using betting progressions because at times the strategy calls for a four-unit bet. If your bet is more than doubled, why take the risky plays such as doubling down against a dealer 9, 10, or Ace?

In the back of Dr. Thorp's *Beat The Dealer*[5] there are some often overlooked tables 4a through 4j. I took a closer look at them and compared the profitability of hitting vs. doubling on hard and soft hands against various dealer up cards. What I came up with is a risk/benefit analysis of doubling down. When you double down, you double your wager but you do not always double your profitability. A couple of examples will demonstrate what I mean. You have a 9-2 vs a dealer eight. If you hit, you have a calculated return of +2153 (or 21.53%). If you double down, doubling your wager, the calculated return increases to +3277. This is a 52% increase in profitability for a 100% increase in risk. Another example would be a 6-5 vs. a dealer 5 up. If you hit, the profitability is +3936, and if you double down it becomes +7873. This is a 100% increase in profitability for a 100% increase in risk.

Using these tables, I developed a somewhat conservative basic strategy for use with progressive betting strategies. The changes were plugged into the computer's program and the data analyzed. This refinement was necessary because what may seem like a logical move, might make a miniscule win rate difference. You might drop your win rate by two percent but nearly double your winnings when doubling down. Additionally, Thorp's strategy was developed for the single deck game and I wanted to develop one for six-deck.

E-Z Basic Strategy was the end product of the analysis. E-Z Basic Strategy was designed for a *six-deck game, double on any two cards, dealer hits a soft 17 and no surrender option*. The house advantage with E-Z Basic Strategy is 0.597%. After about 42 billion hands the strategy was in its final form. Next, I ran 300 billion hands to confirm the data and minimize the error. I had a handful of problem hands which are discussed in Chapter Four. I changed E-Z Basic Strategy to include them and ran another 30 billion hands. The results were analyzed and E-Z Basic Strategy became finalized.

Out of curiosity I ran 50 billion hands of a six-deck game using the same rules as above, but using Thorp Basic Strategy instead. The house advantage jumped to 0.714%. If you are using Thorp Basic Strategy for multi-deck Blackjack, you are giving the house 0.117% extra advantage.

The next testing of E-Z Basic Strategy was done against four-deck Blackjack. If you are wondering why, this is the number of decks used in the continuous shuffling machines. Although rare, you may encounter them and confidence in the strategy you are using is paramount. I ran 150 billion hands of four deck Blackjack using E-Z Basic Strategy and had a house advantage of 0.558%. After this, I ran 50 billion hands of four-deck Blackjack using the Thorp Basic Strategy. The house advantage increased to 0.674%.

Because there are two-deck, hand-tossed games in the casinos where I play, I decided to test E-Z Basic Strategy against two-deck Blackjack. Again, I ran 150 billion hands using E-Z Basic Strategy, and 50 billion hands using Thorp Basic Strategy. E-Z had a 0.550% advantage for the casino. Thorp had 0.546%. This appeared to be the point where the two paths crossed.

Finally, I thought I would see how well E-Z would perform against single deck Blackjack. Surely it would not perform as well as Thorp's strategy because Dr. Thorp's was designed for single deck Blackjack. Again, 150 billion hands were simulated with E-Z and 50 Billion with Thorp. The results were surprising to me because I too considered Thorp to be the single-deck standard. The results were a casino advantage of 0.168% using E-Z and 0.296 using Thorp. The total number of hands ran were 1.022 trillion. E-Z Basic Strategy follows on the next page.

E – Z BASIC STRATEGY

YOUR HAND	DEALER UP CARD									
	2	3	4	5	6	7	8	9	10	A
5-8	H	H	H	H	H	H	H	H	H	H
9	H	D	D	D	D	H	H	H	H	H
10	D	D	D	D	D	D	D	D	H	H
11	D	D	D	D	D	D	D	D	D	H
12	H	H	S	S	S	H	H	H	H	H
13	S	S	S	S	S	H	H	H	H	H
14	S	S	S	S	S	H	H	H	H	H
15	S	S	S	S	S	H	H	H	H	H
16	S	S	S	S	S	H	H	H	H	H
17+	S	S	S	S	S	S	S	S	S	S
A-2	H	H	H	H	D	H	H	H	H	H
A-3	H	H	H	D	D	H	H	H	H	H
A-4	H	H	D	D	D	H	H	H	H	H
A-5	H	H	D	D	D	H	H	H	H	H
A-6	H	D	D	D	D	H	H	H	H	H
A-7	S	D	D	D	D	S	S	H	H	H
A-8	S	S	S	S	S	S	S	S	S	S
A-9	S	S	S	S	S	S	S	S	S	S
AA	SP	SP	SP	SP	SP	SP	SP	SP	SP	SP
22	H	H	SP	SP	SP	H	H	H	H	H
33	H	H	SP	SP	SP	H	H	H	H	H
44	H	H	H	H	H	H	H	H	H	H
55	D	D	D	D	D	D	D	D	H	H
66	SP	SP	SP	SP	SP	H	H	H	H	H
77	SP	SP	SP	SP	SP	SP	H	H	H	H
88	SP	SP	SP	SP	SP	SP	SP	SP	SP	SP
99	SP	SP	SP	SP	SP	S	SP	SP	S	S
10's	S	S	S	S	S	S	S	S	S	S

RED = STAND – S YELLOW = DOUBLE DOWN – D

GREEN = HIT – H BLUE = SPLIT – SP

Let us briefly discuss the major differences between E-Z Strategy and Thorp Strategy. In *hard doubling*, my strategy doesn't double on 9 versus dealer 2 and 11 versus dealer Ace. The dealer 2 is very strong. If you have played before, you know just how often the dealer makes a winning hand from a 2 up. The dealer Ace is extremely strong and seldom busts. The simulations showed these to be the correct moves. You will actually win more with 9 versus dealer 8 up than 9 versus dealer 2 up. The win rate per hour, using a $5 bet, is $0.14 with 9 versus dealer 8 up, and $0.10 with 9 versus dealer 2 up. This demonstrates just how strong a dealer 2 is, and why you should respect it. Hard doubling is such a large part of your winnings (18.762%) that you must get it right.

Soft doubling is also different. Don't double with Ace-2 versus dealer 4 or 5 up, or on Ace-3 versus a dealer 4 up. Simulations once again dictate to hit these. Lastly, I do not double with Ace-6 versus the dealer 2 up.

Other differences are in *pair splitting*. The dealer 2 and 3 are very strong in multi-deck Blackjack so do not split the 2s and 3s against them. Dr. Thorp also splits fours against a 5 up card. Patrick does as well. I found splitting fours to be less profitable. I simply hit the two fours and hope for a ten or eleven card.

After you look over E-Z Basic Strategy, read on. Next we'll discuss how to easily master E-Z Strategy. Start by learning the basic strategy so you will instantly know the right move to make. If followed to the letter, it alone will make you a very competent player.

HOW TO LEARN BASIC STRATEGY

At first glance the basic strategy appears nearly impossible for the average Joe to learn. It's really not.

Start with one area and learn it, then move on to the next. I have color-coded the common moves - standing, hitting, doubling, and splitting - to make learning a visual experience as well.

Hard Standing and Hitting

YOUR HAND

DEALER UP CARD

	2	3	4	5	6	7	8	9	10	A
5-8	H	H	H	H	H	H	H	H	H	H
9	H	D	D	D	D	H	H	H	H	H
10	D	D	D	D	D	D	D	D	H	H
11	D	D	D	D	D	D	D	D	D	H
12	H	H	S	S	S	H	H	H	H	H
13	S	S	S	S	S	H	H	H	H	H
14	S	S	S	S	S	H	H	H	H	H
15	S	S	S	S	S	H	H	H	H	H
16	S	S	S	S	S	H	H	H	H	H
17+	S	S	S	S	S	S	S	S	S	S

The place to start is the hard standing and hitting numbers: 8 or less, 9 through 16, and 17 through 20. With 8 or less, you always hit these versus any dealer up card. With 17 through 20, you always stand versus any dealer up card. With 9, 10, and 11 you have a possible double down and with pairs you have a possible split situation.

The remaining hard hands with totals of 12 through 16 are stiff hands. They aren't good enough to win, but if you hit them, you may bust. Your action is based on the dealer up card. With these hands you stand against dealer up cards 2 through 6 and hit against dealer up cards 7 through Ace. There are two exceptions to the above rule. You should hit a 12 versus dealer up cards 2 or 3. The dealer is very strong with a 2 up card and even though a ten will bust you, you should take a chance because with a 12 you are a sitting duck. The 12 versus the dealer 3 is a closer call but almost all basic strategies say hit it. I ran simulations on these two hands and it confirmed what was thought to be correct. The win rate was higher when hit, and that's the bottom line.

With the second group, 12 through 16 versus dealer 7 through Ace, you must hit all of these. Should you stand, you have a low probability of winning. If you hit, you have a high probability of busting. If you hit these stiff hands you have a chance of making it into a winning hand. This is a situation where you must choose the lesser of two evils: not to win more, but to lose less.

Hard Doubling Down

YOUR HAND					DEALER UP CARD				

	2	3	4	5	6	7	8	9	10	A
9	H	D	D	D	D	H	H	H	H	H
10	D	D	D	D	D	D	D	D	H	H
11	D	D	D	D	D	D	D	D	D	H

When dealt a hand of 9, 10 or 11, you have to decide whether to double down. You may choose to hit them if you already have a large bet out, but knowing when to double down can really increase your winnings. The 10 and 11 are very strong when doubling down, while the 9 is somewhat weaker. An easy way to remember which dealer up cards to double against with the 10 or 11 is to subtract one from each of them. So the 11 would double against a dealer 10 or less, and the 10 would double against a dealer 9 or less. Because the 9 is weaker, only double down with it against a dealer 3 through 6 up. These are the weak dealer hands against your weak 9.

Soft Doubling Down and Other Soft Hands

YOUR HAND					DEALER UP CARD				

	2	3	4	5	6	7	8	9	10	A
A-2	H	H	H	H	D	H	H	H	H	H
A-3	H	H	H	D	D	H	H	H	H	H
A-4	H	H	D	D	D	H	H	H	H	H
A-5	H	H	D	D	D	H	H	H	H	H
A-6	H	D	D	D	D	H	H	H	H	H
A-7	S	D	D	D	D	S	S	H	H	H

If the casino allows you may double down on soft hands. Soft hands are also weak, so again you will only double down against the weaker dealer 3 through 6 up.

Soft hands cannot bust due to the dual value of the Ace, but often you can hit a soft hand and actually make it worse. However, you never stand on the Ace-2 through Ace-6. You always hit or double down these hands. Compared to Thorp's Basic Strategy, many soft double downs were eliminated in E-Z Basic Strategy. You only double Ace-2 against the dealer 6. Ace-3 is doubled against the dealer 5 or 6 up. Ace-4 and Ace-5 are the same: double versus dealer 4, 5 and 6 up. Ace-6 and Ace-7 double versus dealer 3 through 6 up.

The most difficult soft hand to remember how to play is the Ace-7. It's one you may have to memorize because there are three choices. You double down versus dealer 3 through 6, just like A-6. You stand versus dealer 2, 7 and 8 (2 above and 1 below the doubling numbers). Because Ace-7 totals soft 18, and the dealer 9, 10, and Ace are so strong, you hit versus these. My simulations confirm these are the correct moves although some authors may suggest otherwise.

To conclude this section on soft hands, the two remaining soft hands are Ace-8 and Ace-9. These totals are strong enough to win most hands and only a couple of cards could improve them. Always stand on Ace-8 and Ace-9.

Pairs

The final section to learn is pairs. This group has some hard and fast rules regarding splitting, standing and hitting:

1) Always split Aces and 8s.
2) Never split 4s, 5s and 10s.
   A) 4s are more profitable if hit rather than split versus dealer 4, 5 or 6 up.
   B) 5s are best played as a 10, doubling down against a dealer 9 or less.
   C) Possibly the stupidest move in Blackjack would be to split 10s in non-tournament play. I've seen it done.
3) Split 2s and 3s versus dealer 4, 5 or 6 up card. Otherwise, hit.
4) Split 6s versus dealer 6 or less. Otherwise, hit.
5) Split 7s versus dealer 7 or less. Otherwise, hit.
6) Split 9s versus dealer 9 or less with one exception, the 7. The logic here is the dealer has a high likelihood of having a 17 or less, so you are safe standing. Versus the dealer 10 or Ace simply stand.

YOUR
HAND · · · · · · · · · DEALER UP CARD

	2	3	4	5	6	7	8	9	10	A
AA	SP	SP	SP	SP	SP	SP	SP	SP	SP	SP
22	H	H	SP	SP	SP	H	H	H	H	H
33	H	H	SP	SP	SP	H	H	H	H	H
44	H	H	H	H	H	H	H	H	H	H
55	D	D	D	D	D	D	D	D	H	H
66	SP	SP	SP	SP	SP	H	H	H	H	H
77	SP	SP	SP	SP	SP	SP	H	H	H	H
88	SP	SP	SP	SP	SP	SP	SP	SP	SP	SP
99	SP	SP	SP	SP	SP	S	SP	SP	S	S
10's	S	S	S	S	S	S	S	S	S	S

Regarding numbers 4 and 5 above, splitting 6s versus a dealer 7 is a close call, but the profitability chart says hit. Also close is splitting 7s versus dealer 8. Again the chart says hit. The win rate was higher when not split and, as always, profit is the bottom line.

DIFFICULT TO LEARN HANDS

Now let's put together the more difficult to learn parts of the above tables. As you have seen, some of the basic strategy is very easily learned while other parts aren't. Look at the above table for instance.

Aces and 8s are always split
4-4 is always hit
5-5 is treated like a 10
and 10s are never split (poetic isn't it?)

By knowing this, you know half of the above table. The remaining five go into the difficult to learn table along with the other difficult to learn hands.

DIFFICULT TO LEARN HANDS

YOUR HAND   DEALER UP CARD

	2	3	4	5	6	7	8	9	10	A
9	H	D	D	D	D	H	H	H	H	H
12	H	H	S	S	S	H	H	H	H	H
A2	H	H	H	H	D	H	H	H	H	H
A3	H	H	H	D	D	H	H	H	H	H
A4	H	H	D	D	D	H	H	H	H	H
A5	H	H	D	D	D	H	H	H	H	H
A6	H	D	D	D	D	H	H	H	H	H
A7	S	D	D	D	D	S	S	H	H	H
22	H	H	SP	SP	SP	H	H	H	H	H
33	H	H	SP	SP	SP	H	H	H	H	H
66	SP	SP	SP	SP	SP	H	H	H	H	H
77	SP	SP	SP	SP	SP	SP	H	H	H	H
99	SP	SP	SP	SP	SP	S	SP	SP	S	S

In the above table, you see the 9 is doubled against 6 or less except for the strong dealer 2 up card. The 12 only stands against the three weakest dealer up cards, 4, 5 or 6. Remembering the stair-shaped form of soft doubling helps me remember when to double. Again, the soft 18 is difficult so it may have to be memorized. 2-2 and 3-3 are identical. I remember by the saying, " Split 2 and 3 against the 4, 5, 6." Splitting 6s and 7s is easy also. Split 6s against 6 or less. Split 7s against 7 or less. Lastly, as mentioned before, split 9s against 9 or less except for the dealer 7 up.

So what looked like a difficult task is not so bad after all. Learn the E-Z Basic Strategy in this order, practice with cards or computer and soon it will be second nature. After all, it's not brain surgery. Anyone can learn basic strategy with just a little effort. It is the foundation upon which everything else is built.

Problem Hands and Dilemmas

Many of the decisions you need to make are automatic once you master the basic strategy. A quick glance at your cards and the dealers up card and you immediately know exactly what to do. However, some dilemmas do require more contemplation. The contents of your hand, the dealer's up card and the composition of the other players' cards, if visible, need to be considered. Remembering which cards came out the previous round could be helpful as well. Because this can take time, I prefer to be seated at or near third base (the dealer's right). This position does two things for the player. First, you have more time to think about your next play. Secondly, you can see a number of cards and know the order that they came out of the deck. Face up Blackjack allows you to see all cards except the dealer hole card. It lends itself to card observation and card counting.

When using basic strategy and flat betting, you have fewer hard decisions to make. Once you start using a progressive betting system more thought should go into decisions. The odds of making a hand do not change, but the risk does. When you have a one unit bet out and a double down situation presents itself, you can hardly go wrong following a strict basic strategy. However, when you have a four unit bet out, you have lost four hands in a row, four of the last five cards were tens, the previous round was also ten-rich, and the dealer up card is a ten.... As you can see, you need more time to consider whether to double down on your eleven or just hit it. By choosing a seat close to or at third base you have the luxury of time that first base or even second base doesn't have. You also are armed with more information having seen the composition of the cards leading up to your hit and the dealer's draw if he/she needs one.

Let's focus on some problem hands that you will be presented with. In my research, I come across different opinions about how to play many hands. Some authors are very strict basic strategy followers. Others deviate from it and present their logic for doing so. The way I will present this material is to discuss a select group of authors' opinions regarding problem hands and dilemmas. Then I will give my opinion. This may sound like decision by consensus, but one of the benefits of this book is to give you the benefit of many approaches to playing. How to best play a hand is driven by basic strategy, logic and situational analysis. Since I decided to dedicate a chapter to these problems, I ran a 30 billion-hand simulation on the group to confirm my thoughts or confuse the issue even more.

Problem Hand 1: Doubling down on 11 versus Dealer Ace

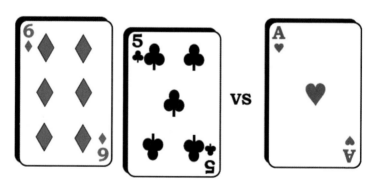

Most authors feel you shouldn't make this move unless you are playing single deck Blackjack. My first impression was not to double in this situation. First, you are going against the most powerful dealer up card, one that has the fewest busts and achieves the highest average score. Second, the profitability is 30%, less than my desired 50%. Third, to beat the dealer Ace you need a 19, 20, or 21. Therefore, you must draw an 8, 9 or 10, the odds of which are still less than 50%. Six out of 13 cards will help, but seven will not. If you hit this one and draw a low card you still have a chance to draw again and make a hand. There are a lot of combinations that can result in a total of 8, 9,or 10.

When I ran the simulations, I found doubling down is no more profitable than simply hitting. The risk is not worth doubling your wager. Every statistic showed it to be essentially even. So if you are strictly playing basic strategy, do not double this one. This is true even playing single deck Blackjack.

If you are using card observation or counting, you are better equipped to make a decision here. Are the 8s, 9s, or 10s due? If so, consider doubling. Were most of the cards just dealt 8s, 9s, or 10s? If so, consider hitting only. If you have been counting cards, what is the count? If the true count is +6, you have a 50-50 chance of drawing a nine or ten. This is why you need to be at third base. You need to take the situation and analyze it. You don't have to always go by the basic strategy cookbook.

Finally, what is your bet? If you are using a progressive betting system, your bet may range from one to four units. You must consider not making high risk moves with higher bets already on the table. You could wipe out an hour's winnings in one wrong move. I will sound like a broken record, but I will say this over and over: play conservatively with large bets out.

Problem Hand 2: Doubling Down 11 versus Dealer 10

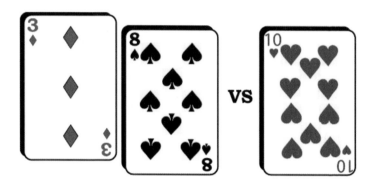

The authors I have read are split on this one. Half say yes and half say no. There are, however, quite a few similarities with situation one. The dealer 10 is still very powerful, with a low bust rate. You still need a 19 or better to win. This means you must draw an 8, 9, or 10, which is still less than 50% odds. The profitability, however, is up to 48%, just under my threshold of 50%.

When I ran simulations using E-Z strategy and changed to doubling down on an 11 versus dealer 10, I saw a 12% improvement in win rate. Units won more than doubled possibly due to fewer pushes. Another thing to consider is the frequency of occurrence. Because the dealer has a high frequency of having a ten up, a small profit is multiplied. To me this is significant. So, because this is so much more profitable, <u>I recommend you double down</u>. The only place you might play it safe is with an extremely high bet out. The win rate in percentage won is the same (47.1%), but if you are uncomfortable with up to eight units bet on one hit, don't double.

Problem Hand 3: Doubling Down on 10 Versus Dealer 9

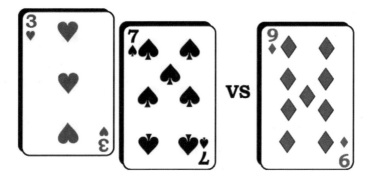

Once again the experts are split 50-50. The dealer strength again decreases, but is still quite strong. You have the same odds of achieving a total of 19 or greater although the cards needed are now 9, 10, or Ace. The win rate is 25% higher when you double down. Therefore, without the benefit of counting and observation, <u>my position is to double down on this one</u>. The simulations confirmed this is the right call and, with progressive betting, the benefits are enough to outweigh the risk.

Problem Hand 4: Doubling Down on 9 Versus Dealer 7

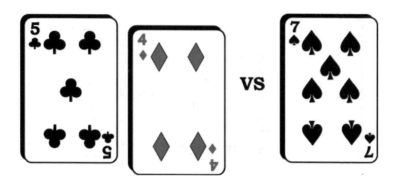

Only one of the experts suggested you make this move. I concur with the majority. Although the dealer 7 is a weak up card, your total is also getting weaker. To achieve a 19 or 20, you must draw a 10 or an Ace. This reduces your odds to about 38% of drawing to 19 or 20. As far as profitability, it is less profitable than hitting. So, <u>do not double on the 9 versus 7</u>. The simulations confirmed this isn't even a close call.

Problem Hand 5: Doubling on 8 Versus Dealer 5 or 6

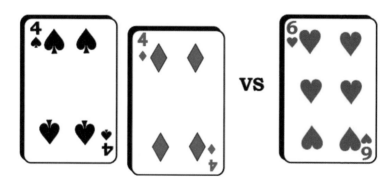

Only two of the experts make this move and one doubled only when playing single deck Blackjack. The bust rate for dealer 5 or 6 is in the low 40% range. Also, you have about a 38% chance of getting an 18 or 19 by drawing an Ace or ten. Given these two factors, it would seem to be a favorable move. Consulting Dr. Thorp's tables, you also see it to be slightly (and I mean slightly) more profitable than hitting. The index was designed for and tested for single deck Blackjack.

My simulations suggest you not double either of these. You will lose much more than you gain. This is another situation that requires you to have a higher probability of getting a ten or Ace to improve the profitability. This can do so in two ways. First, it can help your hand to achieve an 18 or 19 total and, second, a ten would possibly bust the dealer. So, <u>my advice is simply hit the eight</u> unless you are counting cards and the ten count is very positive. You might be able to hit twice, for instance, by drawing a 2 or 3 with the first card.

Problem Hand 6: Splitting Aces Versus Dealer 10

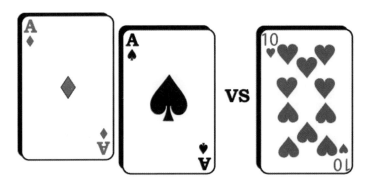

One of the Blackjack rules thought written in stone is "always split 8s and Aces". However, the experts disagree. Again, the split is 50-50. The 10, as you know, is a very strong dealer up card, and if you don't split, you have a 2/12. Another problem is you only get one card. The experts who don't double down on an eleven versus a dealer 10 are also the ones who don't split their aces versus a dealer 10, quite probably for the same reasons.

Drawing to a twelve is not exactly the ideal situation either. I personally would rather be drawing to an eleven. Should you draw to a 12, you need a 9, 8, or 7 to achieve a total of 19 or better. This puts your odds of drawing to 19 or better at about 23% - much lower than drawing to an 11. Another point to consider when splitting the Aces is that one Ace may draw to a winning total and the other may draw to a losing total, making them basically push with the dealer.

The simulations were some help here. The data was almost identical between the two trials, but there was an upward swing in profitability when Aces were split. Also, hands lost were increased when the Aces were not split. This is one case where I feel the pluses seem to outweigh the minuses and I would split my Aces. This goes for splitting Aces versus the dealer Ace up as well. I can say always split 8s and Aces, but you might write it in pencil.

Problem Hand 7: Multi-card 15 or 16 Versus Dealer 7 through Ace up card

The experts generally agree you should hit these totals. The consensus is that you treat this hand just like a two-card total. The odds are the same, right? Well, yes. You are in a tough place here. You probably have a 70% or higher chance of busting. Also, you may have dodged one bullet but you have a bulls-eye painted on your chest now. This is a situation that may be helped by card observation. Look at the last six or so cards that came out. Were they predominantly low cards of the sort that would help you now? If so, you have a high chance of busting by drawing a high card. On the other hand, if a majority of the cards recently dealt are high cards, you might get lucky. With a 16, the Ace, 2, 3, 4, or 5 would improve your situation enough to be competitive. With a 15, the Ace is no help, however, 2, 3, 4, 5, and now 6 will improve your hand. So to at least get a 17, you have 5/13 odds (38.5%) of success. To get a 19 or better, the odds are 3/13. Either way, they are against you. I think your best bet is to use card observation to make the decision. If big cards are due, stand. If small cards are due, hit. Sometimes you have to take a chance.

Problem Hand 8: Surrender

Surrender is a rule that allows the player to forfeit one half of the wager, and end the hand. In other words, the player concedes defeat. It is most often done after the first two cards are dealt.

There is an advantage to having the ability to surrender, but not all casinos allow surrender. If they do, however, it's good to know when to do it. Our experts give some advice when this works to your advantage. Obviously, when you are weak and the dealer is strong is the situation where surrender works to your advantage. It's no surprise you should surrender your 16 versus Dealer 9 through Ace up. Your 15 is also very weak and also should be surrendered to the strong Dealer 9 through Ace (some experts say 10-Ace). Where they divide is whether to surrender your 14 or your pair of 8s. The 14 is weak but 5/13 cards will improve it and 2/13 will make it 15 or 16. In other words, 7/13 will not bust you and 6/13 will. Looking at the experts who opine, they surrender to the dealer Ace.

Some experts also surrender the low cards combination of 5 through 7. They are very weak, but I would not because there are so many combinations that could help you.

To conclude this section, <u>surrender the 15 and 16 versus Dealer 9 through Ace up, and 14 versus Dealer Ace.</u> I would not surrender a pair of 8s but some experts do. I always split a pair of 8s.

Problem Hand 9: Insurance

This is the final dilemma I want to discuss. This is one of the most controversial of calls. I have addressed this previously (p. 9) but I would like to expand on this and tell you what the experts say. Keep in mind, insurance is a side bet and you don't have to

INSURANCE
The bearer of this document is entitled to a settlement equal to two times his or her wager. To be redeemed immediately following the death of said hand.

Cost: one half of wager

POLICY

participate. You can just take what you get, playing out your hand as you normally would.

The odds of a dealer having blackjack are the odds of drawing a ten at any time - 4/13. This is why so many authors agree that taking insurance is a dumb bet. As always, card observation or counting would help you compute the probability of a dealer Blackjack. The only controversy arises when <u>you</u> have Blackjack. If you have Blackjack, you have two choices: 1) Insure or take even money - You will always win something; 2) Not insure - You will win 3:2 over 69% of the time.

Each choice has a valid argument. Let's discuss the arguments. If you insure, you have a bird-in-hand. You will end up with even money either way because insurance pays 2:1 and should the dealer have Blackjack, your hand pushes, but you win the insurance bet. Since you insure for one half of your original bet, you win two times this, which amounts to even money. You come out a winner every time; you just don't get the "premium" of the 3:2 Blackjack payout.

If you do not insure, you are going to push approximately 31% of the time. This will be made up for by the 69% of the time you get the 3:2 payments.

Now, let's look at situations where you are progressing your bets. Let's say you just lost 3 in a row. You would like to stop the bleeding and win, moving you to the winning sequence (see later Chapters Five and Six). To insure is the right call here. If you have lost one hand and you have a one unit bet out (or a one unit bet during the winning sequence), your risk is lower and a push won't hurt you. In other words, you aren't as desperate and the risks/rewards aren't that high.

Here are a few more thoughts regarding this situation. First, a Blackjack is the strongest hand you will ever receive and it would be a shame not to get something for it. Secondly, the frequency of you both having a Blackjack is very low (0.352%), so what happens is probably irrelevant in the long run. Whatever you choose to do is up to you. It's such a close call.

When I ran computer studies, I checked losses from insuring every time. The results were a loss of 7.5% for 77 million insured hands. So 0.075 x 0.352 x $5.00 equals 13 cents per 100 hands. As you can see, it is miniscule.

If you are flat betting you will, in the long run, lose money by insuring your Blackjacks. However, if you are progressing your bets, my advice is to take even money or insure. With the progressive betting systems discussed later, you always want a win to get over to the winning sequence. You are not as dependent on winning double downs, splits or getting Blackjacks, but you are very dependent on keeping your losses to less than five in a row. This is the key to success in using the E-Z Bet system described in Chapter Six. I wouldn't want to push with a Blackjack, and get a stiff on the next hand. Insure your Blackjacks when progressive betting.

Progressive Betting Systems

A betting progression is a sequence of bets designed to improve the return above that of flat betting. The general consensus is there are two ways to win at Blackjack: to count cards or use a progressive betting system. Each has devotees and detractors. One thing in favor of progressive betting is that casinos frown on card counters. You are not going to be barred from a casino for using a progressive betting system. You aren't going to suddenly raise your bet from five dollars to 100 dollars in a progressive system. That's a bit too progressive. As a matter of fact a progressive system will seldom raise a bet more than two units at a time, which isn't going to raise the eyebrow of the dealer, much less the pit boss. What you will see are slow steady wins or losses. Progressive betting is not for the player who wants to strike it rich quickly. Progressive systems are for players who will sit down and play for about an hour at a time, win ten to thirty betting units and quietly leave without being noticed.

This chapter presents systems from a variety of authors, and, many are winners. Your challenge will be to select one that works for you. Sit down with a friend, a deck of cards, and a notebook to try some of them out using one of the basic strategies. As you try them, you will come to realize why you may adjust your strategy to accommodate the higher bets. Mostly, you will hit more of the higher risk double down opportunities rather than doubling down. However, there is beauty in having a three or four-unit bet down and getting an unexpected treat like a ten, eleven or blackjack. In a later chapter I will present an easy formula to evaluate most of the systems mentioned in this book. But for now, let's begin by talking about a system that you want to avoid.

The Martingale

The Martingale is in a category by itself. It is also known as the Small Martingale, to distinguish it from the Grand, or Great Martingale. It is a progressive system that progresses when you lose. For example, you start out by betting a one-unit bet. If you lose the bet, your next bet is two units. If you win, you are up one unit for the two hands. Let's move onto the next level. So you just lost one unit and you get stiffed after you increased the bet to two units, losing them. Your next bet is four units. Should you win, you are up one unit for the three hands. On the surface it seems like a dream come true, but it can turn into a nightmare. Let me burst your bubble: sometimes the dealer will win six, seven or more hands in a row. This will kill your bankroll. See how quickly a $5.00 bet grows:

$5 - $10 - $20 - $40 - $80 - $160 - $320 - $640

So let's say you could bet $640 at your table, how much would you be up if you won this bet? The answer is $5.00. Now the question is, are you going to be the next one to risk $1275 to win $5? I hope you won't try this one. It may work for a while, but the above scenario can and will happen. In a later chapter, I introduce you to the E-Z Bet System that incorporates progressive betting while losing. It is not a true Martingale progression. It only progresses through five levels and really only two bets are doubled up. It is safe and decreases losses compared to flat betting.

Simple Systems

Simple System #1

The first system has probably been around since betting began, but I found it in a book by Richard Harvey, *Blackjack the Smart Way [1999]*[6]. One unit = your minimum bet. A unit could be $5, $25, or more. In units, the system looks like the following:

1 - 2 - 3 - Repeat

This is the winning side of the equation. You start with one unit, and if you win, go to two units. If you win two, go to three units. This is the end of progress. At this point, repeat the sequence until you lose. At any point that you lose, drop to one unit and bet one unit until you win. Then you start the winning progression over again. This is a simple but effective system. The most you can lose is three units unless you double or split.

Harvey recommends you play one unit when:

1] You join the table.
2] The deck(s) is (are) shuffled.
3] A new player joins the table.
4] The cards are bad.

One criticism of this system is you must win three in a row to collect any money from the house. The unit you drag after winning the second bet is your original unit.

My research shows you win three in a row about one out of four series.

Simple System #2

The second simple system is one I came up with to begin dragging after the first win. I have used this successfully and, when the conditions merit, it is a good fall back system. The system is harder to manage at times due to its use of half units. Numerically it looks like the following:

1 - 1 - 1½ - 2 - 3 - Repeat

As with Harvey's system, once you lose, you flat bet one unit until you win. Once you hit the two-unit level, be more conservative.

The advantage to the above system is that after each win you drag part of it rather than letting it all ride. A disadvantage is it will progress at a slightly slower rate. One more note about this system: when the deck seems to be player biased, the sixth bet could be increased to four units, then dropped down. Winning streaks of greater than six in a row are very rare, occurring about two to three percent of the total number of groups.

Simple System #3

The source of the next system is Henry J. Tamburin, from his book, *Blackjack, Take the Money and Run (1994)*.[7] This is about as simple as it gets. There are two levels, small and large bets. The small bet is a one-unit wager that is placed after a loss and continued until you win. The large bet may be two or three units, and is placed after a win and continued until you lose.

Simple System #4

Also from Tamburin, system #4 is a progressive system. Numerically, it looks like the following in units:

1 - 2 - 3 - 5, then back to 1

When you lose, bet one unit until you win. Tamburin and others discuss how a progressive bet falls apart when you have a series of win - lose - win - lose.... During these periods you can lose more than you win because you only win a one-unit bet followed by a two-unit loss. This is referred to as *choppy* and does occur for short periods. It is disheartening when it occurs, but it is the price you pay. The longer winning streaks make up for brief periods of choppiness.

To counter the choppiness, you may flat bet until the period is over, or change to one of the following intermediate systems that compensate for it. The way they compensate is by making the second bet a one-unit bet and, when lost, go to two units on the next hand (see Intermediate Systems #2 and #3).

Simple System #5

This simple system was a late addition to the systems, but a welcome one. The origin for this is the book, *Progression Blackjack,* by Donald Dahl.[8] The book is an enjoyable read. He feels progressive betting is the way to win and the days of counting are numbered. If you haven't guessed, I feel this way too. I think counting for playing decisions is fine, but to vary the bet is almost futile. His betting sequence in units is as follows:

2-2-3-3-4-4-6-6-10-10-14-14-20-20

He gives a progression for $2 to $100 but they all follow the above pattern. He doesn't believe in negative or losing progression. On the losing side he simply flat bets until a win occurs then re-enters the progression above. If you don't believe in counting, then you will enjoy Dahl's book.

This is the last of the simple systems. One thing they have in common is they all flat bet one unit following a loss. The theory is you will lose less if the losing streak lasts very long. In Chapter Six I will look at flat betting more closely to see if this theory is correct. The next group, the intermediate systems, rely on both progressive winning series and deviation from one unit flat betting when in a losing series.

Intermediate Systems

The remaining systems are to start with W (1) and L (1), which stand for the first win after a losing series, and the first loss after a winning series, respectively.

Intermediate System #1

The source of this system is David Popik and his book titled *Winning Blackjack Without Counting Cards (1984).*[9]

Numerically, in units, his system is as follows:

W (1) - 2 - 1 - 1 - 1 ...until lose

L (1) - 1 - 1 - 2 - 1 ...until win

As you can see the system is primarily one-unit bets with strategically placed two-unit bets. Regarding the win side of the progression, Popik states, "This is a typical example of losing out on winning streaks, but these streaks are few and far between".[9] My research shows they aren't that far apart.

Intermediate System #2

In 1983, John Patrick wrote a book titled *So You Wanna Be A Gambler – Blackjack.*[10] This book is a personal favorite and a great book for your collection. Although it was written over 20 years ago, I felt like he wrote it with the same convictions and philosophy that I have today. His basic strategy is conservative, and so is mine. His system is described as "a regression/progression type of wager, rather than an ordinary straight progression method." After the first win, Patrick decreases the wager to one unit. In doing so, he locks in at least a one-unit profit for that series. Should you win the second wager, the system progresses until a loss occurs. On the losing side, he suggests you flat bet two units. The system was designed to profit even during choppy play.

Numerically it looks like the following:

$$W (1) - 1 - 2 - 3 - 3 - 4 - 5$$

$$L (1) - 2 - 2 - 2$$

W (1) is a two-unit starting bet, or is the first win after a losing series. The reason you only see four bets on the loss side is he feels you should quit if you sustain four losses in a row. Patrick labeled this progression the New York system because it starts out 2-1-2, and with the loss bet always at two units, it is always 2-1-2. One of the New York City area codes is 2-1-2, hence the name.

I have only a couple of comments about this ingenious system. Due to the protection of dropping down to one unit, a side effect is you are to the fourth wager before you finally get to a three-unit bet. The net effect is to make this a less volatile and slower progression. Another ingenious characteristic is repeating the 3-unit bet. By doing this you in effect have another lock in of previous winnings. Another observation is should you win two bets then lose two, you will be down by one unit. This system is more aggressive than Popik's. Should you have 4, 5, or 6 wins in a row, you are able to capitalize.

Intermediate System #3

George Pappadopoulos in his book *Blackjack's Hidden Secrets (1999)*[11] introduces his system which he calls the telephone number system. The sequence for winning is to start by betting two units. If you win, drop to one unit. Should you win again, the third bet would go up to two units. The fourth progresses to three units, and the fifth progresses to four units.

Numerically it looks like the following:

2 - 1 - 2 - 3 - 4 - 5, etcetera

The losing sequence is as follows:

2 - 2 - 2 - 2

This is very similar to Patrick's New York system and he acknowledges Patrick for his contribution. He also suggests you hang around for only four losses. On the winning side the only difference is that Patrick repeats the three-unit bet before going up to four units, making the Pappadopoulos system a bit more aggressive but without the second lock in.

This seems to be the appropriate time to discuss the 2-1-2 System. This is a successful system with a logical reason for dropping down to one unit after W (1). However, I think there is more success with a two-unit bet placed there and <u>then</u> drop to one unit. At first glance to drop down to one unit on the second bet seems to be the proper move. However, this is not the only factor. Of the 300 billion hands, 14.33% were double downs and splits. Also, 4.743% were Blackjacks. By placing a two-unit bet when the win rate is 25%, rather than the third bet (at 12% win rate), you double the amount won when doubles, splits and blackjacks occur here. With double the action and high win rates, having a two-unit bet at the second position in effect doubles the win amount.

The following example compares the second spot were you to make bets of five and ten dollars.

$5 or One Unit.........Blackjack pays $7.50
                       Double Down pays $10
                       Split Pair pays $10
                       Win the Hand pays $5

$10 or two Units.......Blackjack pays $15
                       Double Down pays $20
                       Split Pair pays $20
                       Win the Hand pays $10

If this doesn't seem logical to you, stick to the 2-1-2 system. This is a very good system and you can win money with it. It especially works well in choppy play.

You <u>must</u>, at some place, drop to one unit or repeat a bet to have a successful progressive winning sequence. On every hand you have about a 50-50 chance of winning. If you never lock in a win, you always lose greater than or equal to the last bet won. This means you are going to be under 50% without a lock in. Only on prolonged winning streaks will you come out ahead without a lock in. There are a lot of short winning streaks between the prolonged ones. Next I am going to discuss a couple of advanced systems.

Advanced Systems

The advanced systems differ from the intermediate systems by being multi-level or multi-phase. They are more complicated and would be more useful to the professional Blackjack player. They are hard to evaluate for profitability using my simple mathematical formula. They are included for completeness, but not recommended for the beginning average Joe.

Advanced System #1

The first advanced system to discuss was created by Richard Harvey[12] as well. He calls it the 3-Level, Notch-Up, Notch-Down Bet Management System. Level One is a 1-2-3 system where one unit is the basic bet. Should you win all three bets, it's time to notch up to Level Two. Level Two increases the base bet to two units, so it is a 2-3-4 system. In both levels if you lose, you drop to the basic bet for that level. Should you lose again (two in a row) in Level Two you drop down to Level One, base bet. Then as you win, begin progressing through the system again. However, if you continue to lose, stay at the one unit level until things improve. Level Three is a 3-4-5-unit system. When in Level Two, should you progress to and win the four-unit bet, and the table seems very "player friendly," go to Level Three. Begin with a three-unit basic bet and go through the system. If you lose one bet, go to your three unit basic bet for this level. If you lose two in a row, drop back to Level Two, basic bet. I am going to try to diagram the system because it is somewhat complex.

1-2-3 (if you win) 2-3-4 (if you win) 3-4-5

| Level One | Level Two | Level Three |

Should you like an in depth explanation of this system, purchase the book *Blackjack The Smart Way (1999)*. It is well written and is another book you need in your library. Harvey gives some very practical information about some of the more controversial situations you encounter. His information on card observation needs to be read by everyone who plays. I have used it to my benefit when making a critical call on insurance, doubling, and hitting.

Advanced System #2

Jerry Patterson in *Blackjack A Winner's Handbook (2001)*[13] created a four-phase system called Takedown. The first phase is called *Table Evaluation*. In this phase, as the name implies, the table is evaluated for it's dealer or player bias. This can be a brief evaluation but buy in with ten units, have a stop-loss of six units, and play the table minimum. If you win two of three hands and the dealer breaks one of these, you may proceed to phase two.

Phase two is called *Buildup*. During this phase you work your way up from one to five units per level. The system uses a flat bet until three units are won at that level. Starting with one-unit bets, flat bet until you have won three units. They do not have to be consecutive wins and probably won't be. Once you're three units ahead, go to level two with a two unit flat bet. Again bet flat until you are ahead three bets or in this case, six units. This is carried through five levels, to a five-unit bet, with the goal of winning three bets per level. Once all five levels are achieved, you can go to phase three. When a loss occurs during *Buildup*, drop down a level and stay there for one hand. If you win, then go back up. If you lose a second in a row, place one more bet at the lower of the two levels. Should you lose, abort the sequence and leave the table or start again at level one. So, three losses in a row triggers stopping play. This preserves the winnings from the previous levels so you leave the table a winner.

Phase three is called *Score*. Patterson feels if you have gotten this far then you are at a great table and you should cash in, or, as my dad says, "make hay while the sun shines." He introduces a progression system based on the Fibonacci Sequence. Fibonacci was a mathematician in the Middle Ages who came up with a series of numbers called the Fibonacci Sequence. The numbers are one, two, three, five, eight, thirteen, twenty-one... Each number is the sum of the two prior numbers. Patterson suggests you set aside twenty units for this sequence. Starting with one unit, if you win, bet two. If you win, bet three, and on and on. If you lose, move back two levels to get your next bet. Lose two and go back to one unit.

The final phase is called *Takedown*, which stops you from losing back more than a third of your profits from phase three. You simply divide the chips into one third and two thirds. Play with the one third and when they are gone it's time to go. If you keep winning, put aside 2/3 of the winnings and add one third to your playing pile. This way you restrict your losses during *Takedown* to 1/3 of your total.

Proportional Betting

One more technique that I learned and have used to increase winnings is called proportional betting. Credit goes to Henry Tamburin for introducing this in *Blackjack-Take The Money & Run (1994)*.[14] He gives the following example. Say you have a bankroll of $500. During your first session you win $100 using units of $5, so now your bankroll has increased to $600. To use proportional betting you simply increase the unit to $6. This keeps the bankroll to unit ratio at 100 to 1. Now you are betting $6 for one unit, $12 for two units and so on. This is an excellent adjunct to any progressive system, and any bankroll. Use of it can really speed up the rate of winning.

Betting for the Average Joe

The following data comes from my search for a betting system that would be based on hard evidence rather than trial and error. I wanted to develop a system that was profitable, but easy for the average Joe to learn and use. My search led me to ask how frequently a player wins one, two, three, four, five or greater than five wins in a row. I hoped knowing the percentages of each group of wins would help me devise a winning progressive system. It is the basis for the E-Z Bet system that follows. I collected the data using a computer program for high-speed play.

Rules

Six deck shoe
Double on any two cards
Split up to four times
Double after splitting
No surrender or insurance
75% Shoe Penetration
Blackjack pays 3:2
E-Z Basic Strategy

The reason I collected data under the above rules is they are about as strict as you will find. They are also common in the areas in which many of us play. If you find a single deck and/or surrender allowed game, your results should be even be better.

Data

307,409,100,800 hands were played
7,031,609,725 Shoes
Equivalent to 3,002,497,000 Hours of play
Software used: Casino Verite, CVData 3.0

The percentages were broken down into % wins and losses for six categories as follows:

One win followed by a loss
Two wins in a row
Three wins in a row
Four wins in a row
Five wins in a row
> Five wins in a row
One loss followed by a win
Two, three, four, five, and > five losses in a row

Groups of wins or losses in a row

	1	2	3	4	5	>5
%W	51.74	24.89	12.01	5.78	2.8	2.56
%L	43.25	24.80	14.07	7.93	4.48	5.46

Numbers were rounded.

Wins: 133,160,000,000
Losses: 148,030,000,000
% Wins: 43.34
% Loss: 48.16
% Push: 8.50
Ratio W/L: 0.90
Win rate: -0.597%

I also did hand playing and computer playing to come up with some more "casino like" numbers. This will be explained later. Following is the hand played data.

Groups of wins or losses in a row

	1	2	3	4	5	>5
%W	48.9	27.2	13.86	5.05	2.77	2.17
%L	47.23	22.93	15.16	7.87	3.01	3.01

Numbers were rounded.

Wins 1965
Losses 2124
%Wins 48
% Loss 52
Ratio W/L 0.925
W Hands/group 1.95
L Hands/group 2.06

The numbers in the above table were used to develop and evaluate E-Z Bet. These same numbers were used to evaluate the simple, intermediate, and advanced systems from the preceding chapter. This information will be presented in Chapter 7.

I have already discussed why I think the second bet in the winning sequence should be two units. I do agree one should lock in the winnings, but after the second win, not after the first win. After this bet is won, guaranteeing a winning series, you may then progress in either a conservative or aggressive manner. So far it looks like the following:

W (1) - 2 - 1-

Now, let's look back at the table once more. We see that 49 + 27 +14 percent of the time we win either one, two, or three hands in a row. So 90% of the time we never get to the fourth wager. Most of the winning will occur before you get to this point. The one unit bet should be repeated once more before progressing. After the next bet the real gambling in this system begins. I propose two ways to press up your bet - one conservative, and one a bit more aggressive. The conservative way is to pull back one half unit, leaving one and one half units for the next bet. The aggressive way is to press up after the third win, letting the W (3) bet plus winnings ride. Here is what the two sequences look like so far.

CONSERVATIVE

W (1) - 2 - 1 - 1 - 1½ -

AGGRESSIVE

W (1) - 2 - 1 - 2 -

The conscrvative sequence will pull back more of your winnings, making it more profitable. A counter-point to this is that the aggressive system will have greater wins but also greater losses. When you have more money on the table, you will have more profit on the occasions when you receive a Blackjack, double down, split, or just win a long series. Since you have locked in a profit, you are taking a gamble with one unit you just won. You may be able to turn it into a sizeable profit if the winning series continues, or, you will lose one unit trying. Therefore, your style, conservative or aggressive, dictates how you play out the winning series. Here is what the rest of the series looks like.

CONSERVATIVE

$$W\ (1) - 2 - 1 - 1 - 1\frac{1}{2} - 2 - 1$$

AGGRESSIVE

$$W\ (1) - 2 - 1 - 2 - 3 - 4 - 1$$

This carries the sequence out to seven places. Once you arrive here, you have had a good run, and the choice is yours to flat bet one unit or progress more. This completes the winning side of E-Z Bet. Now let's turn our attention to the more complex side - the losing sequence.

The key to winning is to maximize your winnings while minimizing your losses. Turn your attention to the loss percentages. Forty-seven percent of the time you will lose only once and then win the next hand. Conversely, 53% of the time you continue to lose for 2, 3, 4, 5, or >5 losses in a row. You may lose six, seven, eight or more in a row before winning a hand or quitting. Since you never know at what point a losing streak will end, betting high at the beginning of it could be beneficial or could cause you to rack up some high losses before it ends. Let's look at the losing percentages again and design a losing side sequence based on these percentages.

The numbers in the following table were rounded to the nearest whole number.

Groups of losses in a row

	1	2	3	4	5	>5
%L	47	23	15	8	3	3

As you see, 47% of the losses are single losses followed by a win. Since we just lost L (1), which might be one to four units, I suggest you drop down to one unit for the L (2) bet. Your goal for the losing series you just started is to minimize the losses through progressive betting and playing conservatively, trying to keep your losses at no more than four in a row. Greater losing series will happen, but you want to win and stop the losses even if you may have a double down situation. You have to decide if the benefits are worth the risk. For example, suppose that after your third loss in a row you are dealt a six-five, and the dealer up card is an Ace. If you follow the Thorp Basic Strategy, you would automatically double down. But look at E-Z Basic Strategy and you would not.

My advice would be to play the more conservative move and just hit the 11, improving your chance to win the hand. Suppose you doubled and drew an Ace through five. You would be at the mercy of the dealer busting in order to win the hand. It would be more appropriate to play aggressively when in a winning series than during a losing one. The betting sequences which I will introduce later are designed to 1) minimize the losses that occur in losses L (1) through L (4), and 2) not be a session killer by progressing too far or too high in units.

FLAT BETTING

Most people use *flat betting* when in a losing series. Let's look at how much money would be lost when one flat bets based on the percentages above. For demonstration purposes we will use 1½ units as L (1). The L (1) range for the systems in this book is 1.5 to 2.6. What I am going to do is calculate the theoretical amount lost for 100 series lost. Using $5 as a one-unit bet, then L (1) would be $7.50 and L (2) would be $5. L (1) followed by a win yields a loss of $2.50 an average of 47% of the time.

L (1) = - $7.50 + $5 win = - $2.50 x 47% = - $117.50

Next we will calculate the amount lost when L (1) and L (2) are followed by a win.

L (1) + L (2) = - $7.50 - $5 = - $12.50

- $12.50 + $5 win = - $7.50 x 23% = - $172.50

So you see how to calculate the loss during 100 series of losses plus the win that follows. For the purpose of brevity, I am going to put the totals in table form. L (1) W means losing the L (1) bet followed by a win. This applies all the way down the line.

L (1) W	= 47% x	- $2.50	= - $117.50
L (2) W	= 23% x	- $7.50	= - $172.50
L (3) W	= 15% x	- $12.50	= - $187.50
L (4) W	= 8% x	- $17.50	= - $140.00
L (5) W	= 3% x	- $22.50	= -$67.50
L (>5) W	= 3% x	- $27.50	= -$82.50
Total			-$767.50

One would lose $767.50 for 100 losing series when flat betting.

THE MARTINGALE

Now, I am going to suggest a concept that is considered taboo to most authors: **progression of bets when losing**.

The Martingale system of betting was discussed in its classic form in the previous chapter. I tried the classic Martingale system back in 1986 and got burned. I was playing at the Cal-Neva Casino in Reno. The day before, I had won when playing the Martingale system. I figured I would go back and double my previous winnings.

Everything was going well until I found myself head up with a dealer. I was playing at a table with a $200 limit so it was probably a two-dollar minimum. I had won and felt pretty good about my "system." Then I started a losing streak. My fifth bet was $32. I wasn't a big bettor so this was pushing my upper limits. I lost. I knew I would win the next hand so I pushed out the next level, $64. The dealer dealt himself a blackjack. My bankroll was down to about $140, and the next level was $128. I took a big breath and pushed out the bet. What probably started out as a $2 bet had mushroomed to $128 because of the progression. You probably can guess the rest of the story: I lost the hand. What was worse was the dealer again got a blackjack.

I had walked in on top of the world with my winnings of a couple of hundred dollars from the day before and walked out without enough to buy dinner. I haven't used the Martingale system since. If you use it, you too will get burned. However, if both modified and limited, it can prove to be very useful.

E-Z BET LOSING PROGRESSION

The way to modify it is to not try to win the first bet back but to progress to minimize the amount lost to something similar to that of flat betting. The limitation is to progress to the L (5) level and no further. Progressing to the L (6) level increases the maximum bet, but offers no added benefit.

So here is the first of two proposed losing progressions. After your first loss, drop down to a one unit bet for L (2). Should you lose, progress L (3) to one and one-half units. Should you lose, progress L (4) to three units. Should you lose, progress your L (5) bet to six units. This is the end of the progression. Now if you lose L (5), drop to a one-unit bet and ride it out until you win. The whole sequence looks like the following:

$$L (1) - 1 - 1\frac{1}{2} - 3 - 6 - 1 - 1-$$

Now let's calculate the theoretical loss from 100 series of losses just as we did with the flat betting. Again we use -$7.50 as the first loss.

L (1) W	= 47% x	- $2.50	= - $117.50
L (2) W	= 23% x	- $5.00	= - $115.00
L (3) W	= 15% x	- $5.00	= - $75.00
L (4) W	= 8% x	- $5.00	= - $40.00
L (5) W	= 3% x	- $60.00	= -$180.00
L (>5) W	= 3% x	- $65.00	= -$195.00
Total			-$722.50

As you can see, progressing the bet loses less than flat betting. The difference is $45 over 100 series or about 200 hands. Also with a higher bet average, the doubles, splits and Blackjacks will bring even more profit, lessening the losses. For example, when you have four units bet and you get Blackjack. With a flat bet of one unit out, you receive one and a half units. If you have four units bet and get a Blackjack, you receive six units in winnings, a full four times the flat bet payout. This will make a difference in the bottom line with no additional risk. I call this the *Aggressive Losing Sequence*.

Let's look at one other losing progressive sequence. This one has less action and is slightly more conservative. It loses more than the above system but also much less than the flat betting system. Numerically it looks like the following:

L (1) - 1 - 1 - 2 - 4 - 1 - until win

Calculating the losses for 100 series as we did previously is as follows:

L (1) W	= 47% x	- $2.50	= - $117.50
L (2) W	= 23% x	- $7.50	= - $172.50
L (3) W	= 15% x	- $7.50	= - $112.50
L (4) W	= 8% x	- $7.50	= - $60.00
L (5) W	= 3% x	- $42.50	= -$127.50
L (>5) W	= 3% x	- $47.50	= -$142.50
Total			-$732.50

As you can see, this more conservative progressive system, which I call the *Conservative Losing Sequence*, loses $35 less than flat betting. That equals 17.5 cents less per loss. The same advantages exist as above only the bet average drops a bit. So this system in my opinion is a good conservative compromise. The system loses $10 more than the aggressive system. The superiority of a system would depend on when blackjacks or double downs occur. Since there is more action with the aggressive system, random Blackjacks, double downs and splits could easily make it more profitable.

Another way to compare the three systems would be to look at them at different points along the way. After losing one hand and winning the next, with all three systems you would be down $2.50. After losing two hands and winning, flat betting and the conservative system are both down $7.50, but the aggressive system is only down $5.00. After losing three hands and winning, flat betting is down $12.50, the aggressive system is down $7.50, and the conservative system is down $5.00. Finally, after four losses in a row then winning, flat betting is down $17.50, the aggressive system is down $5.00, and the conservative system is down $7.50. After this point, flat betting loses less because of the progression of the other systems.

One more comparison to make is the total amount lost if you were to lose six hands in a row. With flat betting, should you lose six in a row, your total losses are $32.50. With the conservative system, your total would be $52.50. With the aggressive system, your total losses would be $70.00. If your loss limit is $200, you could sustain three or four series of six in-a-row losses before nearing your loss limit. This assumes you don't win between these series. If you were this unlucky, you should quit anyway. If my percentages are correct, you will only experience six or more losses in a row about 3% of the time or once every 33 series. Using one of the progressive systems the rest of the time, your losses will be minimized.

The point of all of these calculations is to point out that there are viable alternatives to flat betting both while winning and losing. Remember, our goal is to maximize winning and minimize losing. Win more and lose less! If you are lucky and have a run where you don't have more than four losses in a row for a while, you will lose very little using either of the two systems above. In the long run you, are better off than flat betting because flat betting will "nickel and dime you to death." Perhaps now limited negative progression will no longer be taboo.

Now let's put them all together. Below are two near optimal winning sequences and two near optimal losing sequences.

Winning Sequences

Conservative

W (1) - 2 - 1 - 1 - 1½ - 2 - 1- until lose

Aggressive

W (1) - 2 - 1 - 2 - 3 - 4 - 1- until lose

Losing Sequences

Conservative

L (1) - 1 - 1 - 2 - 4 - 1- until win

Aggressive

L (1) - 1 - 1½ - 3 - 6 - 1- until win

I encourage you to play conservatively, but don't be a wimp. You know how to play this game, and now, you know how to beat this game. In the next chapter, you will learn how to evaluate the progressive systems we have discussed so far. The evaluations will be put together in a table so you can compare them side-by-side.

Joe, Do the Math

The idea for writing this book came from data kept on over 4000 hands played. I noticed consistent frequencies of groups won in a row. I played with cards and on my computer with a simple Blackjack program. Consolidating the data, I came up with average hands won in a row and lost in a row. The following table was developed.

Groups of wins or losses in a row

	1	2	3	4	5	>5
%W	49	27	14	5	3	2
%L	47	23	15	8	3	3

(Numbers were rounded.)

These percentages are used to evaluate all the systems presented, including my own.

From the 300 billion hands simulated when evaluating E-Z Strategy came a list of the number of hands won or lost in a row. I calculated the percent won and lost in a row and came up with the following table.

Groups of wins or losses in a row

	1	2	3	4	5	>5
%W	52	25	12	6	3	2
%L	43	25	14	8	4	5

(Numbers were rounded.)

Although these results are slightly different from the previous table, they are still close. One reason for the difference is the 4000+ hands are more like actual casino play. The wins in a row are seldom greater than five. Also the losses at the casino seldom exceed five in a row. Many of us would leave the casino if we lost ten hands in a row. But the computer doesn't have that option. It keeps data up to greater than 20 wins and losses in a row. This skews the data to the right. In other words, there were a larger than normal number of high losses in a row. In evaluating the progressive betting systems, I use the data from actual play. For all of you Joes who just want to know the bottom line, proceed to the table at the end of this chapter.

For the rest of you, lets start evaluating the systems. Because we know the frequency that wins occur in a row, we can multiply the amount of units or money times the percentage for that bet and obtain a win rate. The first bet in a series will be followed by a loss of the second bet. This times the percentage will give us an amount won that percentage of the time. Next, we do the second step. This evaluates winning two hands in a row followed by a loss. We continue through the six levels and total the results. Now we have an objective evaluation of a system rather than "testimony" that it works. Perhaps an example will better demonstrate this process.

Simple System # 1

The sequence is 1 - 2 - 3 - 1 - 2 - 3 - 1...

Win (1), lose	= +1-2	= -1x49%	= -49 units
Win (2), lose	= +1+2-3	= 0 x27%	= 0 units
Win (3), lose	= +1+2+3-1	= +5x14%	= +70 units
Win (4), lose	= +1+2+3+1-2	= +5 x 5%	= +25 units
Win (5), lose	= +1+2+3+1+2-3	= +6 x 3%	= +18 units
Win (>5), lose	= +1+2+3+1+2+3 -1	= 11 x 2%	= +22 units
Total units won			= +86 units

The actual number of hands is calculated by multiplying the number of hands per group, 1.95 times 100. So, the 100 series equals 195 hands. 86 units won divided by 195 equals the profit from 195 wins minus 100 losses that followed the series of wins. This is the format I will use to evaluate each system that follows.

The amount lost during every losing series can be computed as well in a similar manner. I simply plug in the Lose (1), win numbers times the percentage for that series and total them up as well. With the above system, the player would simply flat bet one unit until a win occurs. The only problem is to get an average for the first loss. I could estimate, or, I could calculate the value and use the nearest whole number. I estimated it would be about 2 units. My calculator said it is 2.14. So I will use 2 as my average first loss and then calculate the loss side of the series.

Lose (1), win	= -2 +1	= -1 x 47%	= -47 units
Lose (2), win	= -2 -1+1	= -2 x 23%	= -46 units
Lose (3), win	= -2 -1-1+1	= -3 x 15%	= -45 units
Lose (4), win	= -2 -1-1-1+1	= -4 x 8%	= -32 units
Lose (5), win	= -2 -1-1-1-1+1	= -5 x 3%	= -15 units
Lose (>5), win	= -2 -1-1-1-1-1+1	= -6 x 3%	= -18 units
Total units lost			= -203 units

Keep these numbers in mind as I test the other systems. Hopefully they will get better results but they may not. Later in this chapter I will construct a table to show the results side by side. This will demonstrate what causes one system to be better than another. You could even create your own system using the same formula and compare it to the ones listed. I hope to present the most profitable sequence with E-Z Bet, but there are ideas I have not yet tried.

Simple System # 2

The sequence is 1 - 1- 1½ - 2 - 3 - Repeat

Win (1), lose	= +1 -1	= 0 x 49 %	= 0 units
Win (2), lose	= +1 +1 -1.5	= +0.5 x 27%	= +13.5 u.
Win (3), lose	= +1 +1+1.5 -2	= +1.5 x 14%	= +21 u.
Win (4), lose	= +1 +1 +1.5 +2 -3	= +2.5 x 5%	= +12.5 u.
Win (5), lose	= +1+1+1.5 +2+3-1	= +7.5 x 3%	= +22.5 u.
Win (>5), lose	= +1+1+1.5+2+3+1-1	= 8.5 x 2%	= +17 u.
Total units won			= +86.5 u.

Simple System # 3

The sequence is win: 2 units, lose: 1 unit; or win: 3 units, lose: 1 unit

Win (1), lose	= +1 -2	= -1 x 49 %	= -49 u.
Win (2), lose	= +1 +2 -2	= +1 x 27%	= +27 u.
Win (3), lose	= +1 +2 +2 -2	= +3 x 14%	= +42 u.
Win (4), lose	= +1 +2 +2 +2 -2	= +5 x 5%	= +25 u.
Win (5), lose	= +1 +2 +2 +2 +2 -2	= +7 x 3%	= +21 u.
Win (>5), lose	= +1 +2 +2 +2 +2 +2 -2	= +9 x 2%	= +18 u.
Total units won			= +84 u.

The total for three units is exactly the same as for two.

Simple System # 4

The sequence is 1- 2 - 3 - 5 - 1 - 1 - 1...

Win (1), lose	= +1 −2		= -1 x 49 %	= -49 units
Win (2), lose	= +1 +2 -3		= 0 x 27%	= 0 units
Win (3), lose	= +1 +2 +3 -5		= +1 x 14%	= +14 units
Win (4), lose	= +1 +2 +3 +5 -1		= +10 x 5%	= +50 units
Win (5), lose	= +1 +2 +3 +5 +1 -1		= +11 x 3%	= +33 units
Win (>5), lose	= +1 +2 +3 +5 +1 +1 -1		= +12 x 2%	= +24 units
Total u. won				= +72 units

Simple System #5

The sequence is 2 - 2 - 3 - 3 - 4 - 4 - 6.... It goes out to ten units but to evaluate I only need it out to seven places.

Win (1), lose	= +2 -2		= 0 x 49 %	= 0 units
Win (2), lose	= +2 +2 -3		= +1 x 27%	= +27 units
Win (3), lose	= +2 +2 +3 -3		= +4 x 14%	= +56 units
Win (4), lose	= +2 +2 +3 +3 -4		= +6 x 5%	= +30 units
Win (5), lose	= +2 +2 +3 +3 +4 -4		= +10 x 3%	= +30 units
Win (>5), lose	= +2 +2 +3 +3 +4 +4 -6		= +12 x 2%	= +24 units
Total u. won				=+167 units

Keep in mind the units above have doubled, and the bet when losing is also a 2 unit flat bet. Let's examine that. The L (1) bet is going to average a little more than 2 units- 2.33 to be precise. Since it rounds down to 2 units that is what I will use.

Lose (1), win	= -2 +2		= 0 x 47%	= 0 units
Lose (2), win	= -2 -2 +2		= -2 x 23%	= -46 units
Lose (3), win	= -2 -2 -2 +2		= -4 x 15%	= -60 units
Lose (4), win	= -2 -2 -2 -2 +2		= -6 x 8%	= -48 units
Lose (5), win	= -2 -2 -2 -2 -2 +2		= -8 x 3%	= -24 units
Lose (>5), win	= -2 -2 -2 -2 -2 -2 +2		= -10 x 3%	= -30 units
Total u. lost				= -208 units

Intermediate System # 1

I will evaluate both winning and losing sequences for the intermediate systems.

Winning sequence: W (1) - 2 - 1 - 1 - 1 - 1 - 1...

Losing sequence: L (1) - 1 - 1 - 2 - 1 - 1 - 1... where L (1) = 1.5 units.

Win (1), lose	= +1 -2	= -1 x 49 %	= -49 u.
Win (2), lose	= +1 +2 -1	= +2 x 27%	= +54 u.
Win (3), lose	= +1 +2 +1 -1	= +3 x 14%	= +42 u.
Win (4), lose	= +1 +2 +1 +1 -1	= +4 x 5%	= +20 u.
Win (5), lose	= +1 +2 +1 +1 +1 -1	= +5 x 3%	= +15 u.
Win (>5), lose	= +1 +2 +1 +1 +1 +1 -1	= +6 x 2%	= +12 u.
Total units won			= +94 u.

Lose (1), win	= -1.5 +1	= -0.5 x 47%	= -23.5 u.
Lose (2), win	= -1.5 -1 +1	= -1.5 x 23%	= -34.5 u.
Lose (3), win	= -1.5 -1 -1 +2	= -1.5 x 15%	= -22.5 u.
Lose (4), win	= -1.5 -1 -1 -2 +1	= -4.5 x 8%	= -36 u.
Lose (5), win	= -1.5 -1 -1 -2 -1 +1	= -5.5 x 3%	= -16.5 u.
Lose (>5), win	= -1.5 -1 -1 -2 -1 -1 +1	= -6.5 x 3%	= -19.5 u.
Total u. lost			=-152.5 u.

Upon looking at these numbers, one can see the winnings are up, based on a one unit starting wager, and the losses are down. Once you factor in payoffs from Blackjack, doubles and splits, this system should be close to even.

Intermediate System # 2

Winning sequence: 2 - 1 - 2 - 3 - 3 - 4 - 5...

Losing sequence: 2 - 2 - 2 - 2

    The inventor of this sequence quits if he experiences 4 losses in a row, so the loss evaluation can only proceed out that far.

Win (1), lose	= +2 -1	= +1 x 49 %	= +49 u.
Win (2), lose	= +2 +1-2	= +1 x 27%	= +27 u.
Win (3), lose	= +2 +1 +2 -3	= +2 x 14%	= +28 u.
Win (4), lose	= +2 +1 +2 +3 -3	= +5 x 5%	= +25 u.
Win (5), lose	= +2 +1 +2 +3 +3 -4	= +7 x 3%	= +21 u.
Win (>5), lose	= +2 +1 +2 +3 +3 +4 -5	= +10 x 2%	= +20 u.
Total u. won			= +170 u.

Lose (1), win	= -2 +2	= 0 x 47%	=	0 units
Lose (2), win	= -2 -2 +2	= -2 x 23%	=	-46 units
Lose (3), win	= -2 -2 -2 +2	= -4 x 15%	=	-60 units
Lose (4), Quit	= -2 -2 -2 –2 Quit	= -8x 8%	=	-64 units
Total units lost				= -170 units

    This isn't completely accurate since it isn't carried out past four losses, but we'll go with it. If you chose not to leave and played 2 units out to seven places, it would be identical to the table for simple system 5, 208 units. You should find that you lose 4 or more in a row approximately 14% of the time, or, one in seven series. This means you will be looking for a new table quite often. However, looking at the numbers, they are now even. I hope that some of the future systems will actually win more than they lose. Again, factor in blackjacks, doubles and splits and this system does just that.

Intermediate system # 3

Winning sequence: 2 - 1 - 2 - 3 - 4 - 5 - 6...

Losing sequence: 2 - 2 - 2 - 2

Win (1), lose	= +2 -1	= +1 x 49 %	= +49 u.
Win (2), lose	= +2 +1-2	= +1 x 27%	= +27 u.
Win (3), lose	= +2 +1 +2 -3	= +2 x 14%	= +28 u.
Win (4), lose	= +2 +1 +2 +3 -4	= +4 x 5%	= +20 u.
Win (5), lose	= +2 +1 +2 +3 +4 -5	= +7 x 3%	= +21 u.
Win (>5), lose	= +2 +1 +2 +3 +4 +5 -6	= +11 x 2%	= +22 u.
Total u. won			= +167 u.

The losing sequence is the same as the above, -170 units, or 208 units if carried out to L (>5), W. The system is virtually identical to #2. The #2 system is slightly more profitable due to the repeated 3-unit bet. This is in effect another lock-in just as the one unit bet is.

Advanced System #1

The winning side of this one is probably a bit easier to analyze than the losing side. The winning sequence is as follows:

1- 2 - 3 - 2 - 3 - 4 - 3 - 4 - 5...

Win (1), lose	= +1 -2	= -1 x 49 %	= -49 units
Win (2), lose	= +1 +2 -3	= 0 x 27%	= 0 units
Win (3), lose	= +1 +2 +3 -2	= +4 x 14%	= +56 units
Win (4), lose	= +1 +2 +3 +2 -3	= +5 x 5%	= +25 units
Win (5), lose	= +1 +2 +3 +2 +3 -4	= +7 x 3%	= +21 units
Win (>5), lose	= +1 +2 +3 +2 +3 +4 -3	= +12 x 2%	= +24 units
Total u. won			= +77 units

One thing to note is, with this advanced system, one does not always enter the sequence at 1 unit. For instance, if you won five in a row, the next bet would be 4 units. If lost, the bet to follow would be 2 units, which is the basic unit for that level. If you only lose the 4-unit bet and win the 2-unit bet, you would start the next winning series there, rather than at one unit. The next series would look like the following:

2 - 3 - 4 - 3 - 4 - 5 - 5...

The last 5-unit bet is presumed, as Harvey did not give any more numbers above 5 units. Now lets calculate this winning sequence.

Win (1), lose	= +2 -3	= -1 x 49 %	= -49 u.
Win (2), lose	= +2 +3 -4	= +1 x 27%	= +27u.
Win (3), lose	= +2 +3 +4 -3	= +6 x 14%	= +84 u.
Win (4), lose	= +2 +3 +4 +3 - 4	= +8 x 5%	= +40 u.
Win (5), lose	= +2 +3 +4 +3 +4 - 5	= +11 x 3%	= +33 u.
Win (>5), lose	= +2 +3 +4 +3 +4 +5 - 5	= +16 x 2%	= +32 u.
Total u. won			= +167 u.

As you can see the profits go up more than double the earlier sequence. The number of units bet goes up also. From W (2) on the profits soared.

I am going to attempt to analyze this system's losing side, but it is very difficult. For one thing, the losing amount varies depending on where the first loss is in the sequence. I picked a couple of starting points to see how they compared. The way the system works is if you lose at any point you drop to the lowest bet in that level. For example, you are in level 2, which starts with 2 units and goes to 4 units. After a loss anywhere in this level you would go to 2 units for the next bet. Should you lose again, you would go to level 1 basic bet which starts at one unit. So, I picked level 2, 3 units to start the losing sequence. Now let's see what it looks like.

Lose (1), win	= -3 +2	= -1 x 47%	= -47 units
Lose (2), win	= -3 -2 +1	= -4 x 23%	= -92 units
Lose (3), win	= -3 -2 -1+1	= -5 x 15%	= -75 units
Lose (4), win	= -3 -2 -1 -1 +1	= -6 x 8%	= -48 units
Lose (5), win	= -3 -2 -1 -1 - 1+1	= -7 x 3%	= -21 units
Lose (>5), win	= -3 -2 -1 -1 - 1 -1 +1	= -8 x 3%	= -24 units
Total u. lost			= -307 units

This looks like a bad place to enter the sequence for an evaluation of losses. I did a second test starting at level one, 2 units, and the losses were only 203 units. This is much better and is the same as flat betting because you follow the 2-unit bet with one-unit bets until you win. I also ran a test at a higher level and had a correspondingly higher loss level. Fortunately, you have to win more to get up to the higher level. I averaged the three and got -309 units.

Advanced System #2, Takedown

Phase two, *Buildup*, is flat betting at five different levels. Once 3 bets at one level have been won, you then move up a level and win three more, move up and so forth. The goal is to win 3 bets at each of the five levels. If you lose, drop down a level - say from 3 units to 2 units. Win at that level and go back up. Lose a second time, place a second bet at the lower level. Lose this one and quit the table or start over at level one. I cannot evaluate this complex system with my simple formula.

A way to evaluate the losing side is to pick an arbitrary point to have the first loss and follow the instructions. Unfortunately, if you quit after 3 losses, the evaluation ends there. If you play on, you would go down to one unit and stay there until a win occurs. This scenario we can evaluate. I am going to show one sequence then simply list the rest for brevity. This losing sequence starts at level 3 where the first loss occurs.

Lose (1), win	= -3 +2	= -1 x 47%	= -47 units
Lose (2), win	= -3 -2 +2	= -3 x 23%	= -69 units
Lose (3), win	= -3 -2 - 2 +1	= -6 x 15%	= -90 units
Lose (4), win	= -3 -2 - 2 -1 +1	= -7 x 8%	= -56 units
Lose (5), win	= -3 -2 - 2 -1 - 1+1	= -8 x 3%	= -24 units
Lose (>5), win	= -3 -2 - 2 -1 - 1 -1 +1	= -9 x 3%	= -27 units
Total u. lost			= -313 units

Somewhat like advanced system #1, the amount lost per 100 series of losses would depend on where you pick along the 15 bets (5 levels x 3 bets per level). More will be lost from the higher levels, but more was won for you to get there. The following table gives the results for losing at all 5 levels and the average of the 5.

Level 1 - 104 units
Level 2 - 203 units
Level 3 - 313 units
Level 4 - 433 units
Level 5 - 533 units
Average: - 317 units

E-Z Bet

I will look at both the winning sequences before going to the losing sequences.

Conservative winning sequence:

W (1) - 2 - 1- 1 - 1½ - 2 - 1...

Win (1), lose	= +2 -2	= 0 x 49 %	= 0 u.
Win (2), lose	= +2 +2 -1	= +3 x 27%	= +81 u.
Win (3), lose	= +2 +2 +1 -1	= +4 x 14%	= +56 u.
Win (4), lose	= +2 +2 +1 +1 -1.5	= +4.5 x 5%	= +22.5 u.
Win (5), lose	= +2 +2 +1 +1 +1.5 -2	= +5.5 x 3%	= +16.5 u.
Win (>5), lose	= +2+2+1+1+1.5 +2 -1	= +8.5 x 2%	= +17 u.
Total u. won			=+193 u.

Aggressive winning sequence:

$$W (1) - 2 - 1 - 2 - 3 - 4 - 1...$$

Win (1), lose	= +2 -2	= 0 x 49 %	= 0 u.
Win (2), lose	= +2 +2 -1	= +3 x 27%	= +81 u.
Win (3), lose	= +2 +2 +1 -2	= +3 x 14%	= +42 u.
Win (4), lose	= +2 +2 +1 +2 -3	= +4 x 5%	= +20 u.
Win (5), lose	= +2 +2 +1 +2 +3 -4	= +6 x 3%	= +18 u.
Win (>5), lose	= +2 +2 +1 +2 +3 +4 -1	= +13 x 2%	= +26 u.
Total u. won			=+187 u.

What is going on here? I risk more, aggressively betting, and I don't win as much. That doesn't make sense! It does if you look at what happens when you are betting bigger at the W (3) and W (4) levels. When you lose, you lose more, taking away from your previous winning hands. These are multiplied by the higher percentages at 3 and 4 as well. The units will be recaptured at the W (>5) level but at such a low percentage that you can't recover. One saving grace is the higher average bet in the aggressive sequence. This will yield big dividends as usual when one gets a blackjack, splits, and double downs. This is what makes this more aggressive and not the bottom line above. Now let's look at the losing betting progression. In the previous chapter I demonstrated the win rate using $5 units. Now I will do the same using units (which will be easier to compare to the other systems).

Aggressive losing sequence: L (1) - 1- 1½ - 3 - 6 - 1 - 1...

Lose (1), win	= -1.5 +1	= -0.5 x 47%	= -23.5 u.
Lose (2), win	= -1.5 -1 +1.5	= -1 x 23%	= -23 u.
Lose (3), win	= -1.5 -1 -1.5 +3	= -1 x 15%	= -15 u.
Lose (4), win	= -1.5 -1 -1.5 -3 +6	= -1 x 8%	= -8 u.
Lose (5), win	= -1.5 -1 -1.5 -3 -6 +1	= -12 x 3%	= -36 u.
Lose(>5),win	= -1.5-1-1.5 -3 -6-1+1	= -13 x 3%	= -39 u.
Total lost			= -144.5 u.

Conservative losing sequence: L (1) - 1 - 1- 2 - 4 - 1 - 1...

Lose (1), win	= -1.5 +1	= -0.5 x 47%	= -23.5 u.
Lose (2), win	= -1.5 -1 +1	= -1.5 x 23%	= -34.5 u.
Lose (3), win	= -1.5 -1 -1 +2	= -1.5 x 15%	= -22.5 u.
Lose (4), win	= -1.5 -1 -1 -2 +4	= -1.5 x 8%	= -12 u.
Lose (5), win	= -1.5 -1 -1 -2 -4 +1	= -8.5 x 3%	= -25.5 u.
Lose (>5), win	= -1.5 -1-1-2-4-1+1	= -9.5 x 3%	= -28.5 u.
Total lost			= -146.5 u.

What's going on here? I bet more but lose less! Look back at the last chapter.

Flat Bet

It is a fair question to ask what would happen if I just flat bet all the time. To compare this to a two unit base system, multiply the results by two. This would result in 184 units won and 208 units lost.

Win (1), lose	= +1 -1	= 0 x 49 %	= 0 u.
Win (2), lose	= +1 +1 -1	= +1 x 27%	= +27 u.
Win (3), lose	= +1 +1 +1 -1	= +2 x 14%	= +28 u.
Win (4), lose	= +1 +1 +1 +1 -1	= +3 x 5%	= +15 u.
Win (5), lose	= +1 +1 +1 +1 +1 -1	= +4 x 3%	= +12 u.
Win (>5), lose	= +1 +1 +1 +1 +1 +1 -1	= +5 x 2%	= +10 u.
Total u. won			= +92 u.

Lose (1), win	= -1 +1	= 0 x 47%	= 0 u.
Lose (2), win	= -1 -1 +1	= -1 x 23%	= -23 u.
Lose (3), win	= -1 -1 -1 +1	= -2 x 15%	= -30 u.
Lose (4), win	= -1 -1 -1 -1 +1	= -3 x 8%	= -24 u.
Lose (5), win	= -1 -1 -1 -1 -1 +1	= -4 x 3%	= -12 u.
Lose (>5), win	= -1 -1 -1 -1 -1 -1 +1	= -5 x 3%	= -15 u.
Total u. lost			= -104 u.

Now let's put the results together.

System	Win Tot.	Lose Tot.	Net +or-	Avg. Bet:	Net/Bet
Sim. 1	+86	-203	-117	2.14	-54.7
2	+86.5	-203	-116.5	1.83	-63.7
3	+84	-203	-119	2.00	-59.5
4	+72	-203	-131	2.59	-50.6
5	+167	-208	-41	2.65	-15.5
Int. 1	+94	-153	-58.5	1.49	-39.3
2	+170	-170	0	1.82	0
3	+167	-170	-3	1.92	-1.6
Adv. 1	+77	-203	-126	2.40	-52.5
2		-203			
Con E-Z	+193	-147	+46.5	1.54	+30.2
Agr. E-Z	+187	-145	+42.5	1.82	+23.4
Flat Bet	+92	-104	-12	1.00	-12

Red highlighted areas are probably best avoided.
Yellow highlighted areas are close to zero, or neutral.
Green highlighted areas are positive.

Let's look at the above table. Win total and lose total were taken from the previous calculations. The net is the difference between the win and lose totals. The average bet was calculated from the above tables. The net/bet column is my way of leveling the playing field among the various systems, since there is a great deal of variability there.

The yellow and green highlighted lines are ones that either come close to even or are positive. Remember that intermediate systems 2 and 3 stopped their loss bets at four in a row. This can be looked at as a smart move on their part, but makes comparing the data difficult. Were you to carry their 2-unit bet on out to seven places, the loss number would be much higher (208 units). Also note that flat betting performs better than a lot of the systems. With a few blackjacks and double downs, you could have an even game. If you double the win rate for flat betting, using a 2-unit wager, the win total would be 184, which is not bad. The problem is, when this is done, it affects the loss side, increasing the losses to near double as well due to the higher L (1).

Look once more at the last table. Five systems reduce the losses. Two of these do it by leaving the table after four losses. The other three have one thing in common: some form of negative progression. Intermediate System #1 uses a negative progression in only one spot, the L(4) position and reduces the losses from a flat rate loss of about 203 units to 152.5. This is achieved with only increasing the wager by one unit above a flat bet. I think this is remarkable for such a small change. Were you to combine this losing sequence with a more aggressive winning sequence one might see good performance. Finally note that the difficulty of analysis makes it hard to evaluate the advanced systems.

The only systems that came out with positive net wins were the E-Z bet systems. They could be matched with other systems and make them more profitable. For instance, match Intermediate 2 or 3 winning sequence with either of the E-Z loss sequences and both would be in the plus column. Match Simple System 5 with E-Z loss sequences and it also goes to the plus side. Match the E-Z conservative winning sequence with the E-Z aggressive loss sequence and you have a slightly more profitable combination. Other winning sequences and losing sequences may be combined to create a winning combination.

If you must count...

This book has been written for the average Joe who doesn't want to learn a counting system. It contains a number of progressive betting systems. Although I believe you can use them to become a winner, you have the ability to enhance your betting and playing decisions. You can't have too much information when playing Blackjack. If you knew the odds were against receiving a nine, ten or Ace, would you double down or hit that ten? You would simply hit it.

You could improve your odds by learning one of the multitudes of counting systems. You might get a percent on the house. That isn't much, but I guess it beats nothing. Of course they take much time and dedication to master. Once mastered, they are not an exact science. They merely tell you there is a more favorable or less favorable situation. If you knew the last four cards in the deck were three tens and a six, would you know you would get the two tens? Or would you get the ten-six?

I'm not even sure card counting works any more. The people who run casinos are no dummies. They can hire the smartest people in the world if they want them. They have instituted countermeasures that are very hard to beat. It's hard to find a single deck game anymore.

Where I play, it's six decks. They burn cards, use machines to shuffle and shuffle up early. They have sophisticated security with face recognition software. They have pictures of every known card counter. They're suspicious of everyone. They look for people who are paying close attention to what's being dealt. They are looking for big jumps in your betting after an hour of flat betting the minimum. **They're looking for you. They don't like you, Mr. Card Counter.**

I even ran some simulations using the common rules: six decks, double on any two cards, dealer hits a soft 17. You know what? Flat betting and playing basic strategy beat the counting systems hands down. So, I don't put a lot of stock in counting cards. Besides, I play to have a good time and if I have to work that hard, I'd rather be at work.

Card counting tells you less than simply scanning the table. I first read about card observation in *Blackjack The Smart Way,* by Richard Harvey[15]. For a complete discussion, read his book. For now, let me give a brief reflection. Card observation is a technique of scanning the cards just played in an attempt to determine the dealer hole card and your next hit possibilities. By observing the cards leading up to the hole card, you try to guess the hole card. This may come in handy if you have a difficult decision to make. It may be used to decide to take insurance or not. It may be useful when deciding to double down or just hit. The same holds true for knowing what you might get if you draw. By sitting at third base, you will be able to see the cards your fellow players draw. The composition leading up to your play may affect your decision to hit that stiff or stand. It may help you to determine if you should double down or hit. I personally have used this technique. It works.

A further advantage may be obtained by knowing if the ten-composition is positive or not. When you know the large cards are more concentrated in the remaining decks, you are armed with another weapon. Combined with card observation, perfect basic strategy, and a good progressive betting system, you are well equipped to win.

An easy way to estimate the concentration of tens is to use **E-Z Count**. Although I call it a counting system, this system is a ten-tracking system: simply a way of estimating if the deck is favorable for certain plays. When you enter play at a Blackjack table, they don't put blinders on you. You shouldn't put them on yourself either.

So what is E-Z Count? E-Z Count is a way to track tens by subtracting the number of tens played in a round from the number of players' hands. You use hands played rather than the number of players, because some hands are split and some players play more than one hand. For example, at a table with four players, all playing one hand, one should expect to see four tens to be dealt. Should only two of the four be dealt, the count would be plus two. Should six tens come out, four minus six equals minus two. One would then carry this count over to the next hand. Early in a six-deck shoe, the count would probably be irrelevant. As time goes by, and more decks have been played, the count will become usable.

If familiar with counting systems, you know that with greater than one deck of cards, you must compensate for the difference between the running count and the true count. A *running count* is the cumulative count since the shuffle. A *true count* is obtained by dividing the running count by the number of decks remaining in the shoe. Let's say the running count is plus eight and the discard tray shows that about two decks of a six-deck shoe have been played. This means there are still four decks to be played. To obtain the true count we now divide the running count, plus eight, by four and we get plus two. Two is the true count. This allows you to always compare apples to apples.

What a true count of plus two means is that for each of the remaining 52 card decks, there are two extra tens. So now there are 18-tens and 34 non-tens. The proportions have improved but not enough to make any major moves regarding perhaps increasing your bet. If the true count went up to four you might be able to increase your winnings by increasing the unit value while using the same betting system. I think you are better off to use a good progressive betting system and use the information for playing decisions.

If you have a true count of four or greater, you must consider this information in playing. You can now double down more confidently. Your assumption of a dealer hole card of ten is more accurate now. You are going to have a better chance of receiving a Blackjack now. The dealer has a higher bust rate with a 2 through 6 up card. You also have a higher bust rate when hitting your stiff hands. By using a counting system, you open up your game to deviations from the basic strategy. Keeping some sort of count offers many advantages. This is just a little more ammo to add to your arsenal.

The way E-Z count was derived is based on the average number of cards per hand. I had previously read the average number of cards per hand is 2.5. As stated earlier, when running statistics on E-Z Basic Strategy, I ran over 300 billion hands. I found that the figure is exactly 2.75 cards per hand. Let's use our example of four players/hands plus the dealer's hand to see if E-Z Count is accurate.

Five Hands x 2.75 cards/hand = 13.75 cards dealt.
The tens compose 30.77% of the deck.
13.75 x 0.3077 = 4.23 tens should be dealt.
Rounded off this equals 4 tens: the number of players.

Do this for two through seven hands and you will find the following:

1.69 tens for two hands/one player
2.53 tens for three hands/two players
3.38 tens for four hands/three players
4.23 tens for five hands/four players
5.07 tens for six hands/five players
5.92 tens for seven hands/six players

As you can see, for three to six players, the system is pretty accurate. It will give you an idea of whether the deck is ten rich, neutral, or ten poor. I think it is accurate enough to be used for playing decisions, especially if the true count were to get as high as three or four. If you were off by one, the true count would be two or three. Even if you are using card observation, you can use E-Z Count to judge if the correct proportion of ten cards were showing.

This is so easy to do you shouldn't consider it counting, just tracking tens. A quick glance and a quick subtraction and you have a quick count. Carry this over from hand to hand and adjust the running count to a true count. If it is three or four, look for more tens. If it is negative, drop your unit value or if playing a betting progression, play more conservatively. If you are using E-Z Bet, you could use the count to tell you to switch between the aggressive and conservative sequences.

The E-Z Count is not an exact counting method. Neither is any system that requires one to "estimate" the number of cards discarded. You are never exact unless you are playing single deck Blackjack. E-Z Count is not unlike the Thorp Ten Count. Dr. Thorp[16] counted tens and others. He then divided the others, or non-tens, by the tens and got a ratio. Using this ratio, he determined his bet in units. When the ratio was above 2.00, he stayed at one unit. Between 2.00 and 1.75, he would bet two units. Between 1.75 and 1.65, the bet went to four units, and below 1.65, five units. This system was designed for single deck Blackjack, but it could easily be adapted to six decks. You would just have to start with 216 others divided by 96 tens and count down from there. This is pretty easy for all of you PhDs. As for this average Joe, I think I'll stick with E-Z Count.

Money Management

Have you ever won a considerable amount of money only to lose it back? Have you ever said, if only I had quit while I was ahead? How did you feel? More than likely your feelings were disgust, anger, and disbelief that you could not walk away from the table a winner. You are not alone. This has happened to every gambler at one time. Today, it has happened for the last time.

This brings to mind that big fish I hooked. Man, what a fight he put up. He was big enough to have mounted and hung on the wall in my den. You know, I had him where I wanted and as I reached down to grab him, he got away. You should have seen him. What a fish! Are you tired of having the "fish" hooked, only to let it get away?

It doesn't matter how much you were up, it's how much you had when you left the table that counts. You may have been up a grand, but walked out down $400. You still lost, but, my friend, you are not a loser. When you were up that grand, you had just achieved a position few people achieve. You were a winner at that moment. You didn't manage your winnings well and you haven't developed the discipline to know when to quit. Let's listen to some sage advice on the subject.

- John Patrick[17] states, "Without money management, you can't be a consistent winner."

- George Pappadopoulos[18] states of his five rules, "If I were to pick only one, as being the most important, it would be money management."

- Avery Cardoza[19] states "Money management and emotional control are the centerpiece of any winning strategy."

Does this drive home the importance of money management?

Money management and discipline are so closely aligned that I have rolled the two together. Some authors include progressive betting systems to be part of money management, which it is, but I chose to discuss it separately. Money management includes proper bankroll, purchasing chips, stacking chips, keeping up with where you stand, setting win limits, and setting loss limits. Discipline comes from within. Advice can be given about what to do and what not to do. You must develop the discipline to carry out what you know you should do. You can!

Note: The following examples use a $5 unit bet. If your base bet is higher, simply adjust accordingly.

Bankroll

Most authors agree that a bankroll for one session (sitting) of blackjack should be forty times your base bet (unit). What this means is if your base bet is $5, then for that session you should have available $200. If you are planning to play three sessions that day, have $600 available for the day, but only take $200 to the table at any one time. This becomes a protection for you should you have a run of very bad luck. Do not confuse this with your session loss limit. Your session bankroll and your session loss limit are two different things. The $200 is to allow you to have enough reserve to capitalize when an opportunity arises such as doubling down after splitting. Also, by taking only $200 of your stake, you are assured of having at least two more sessions. Take it all and you might be tempted to risk it all. If you do, you will also risk only having one session.

Chips

Do not purchase $200 in chips as soon as you walk up to the table. You should start with half. One reason you only purchase half is more psychological than practical. You will have to pause when you reach into your pocket and pull out the last $100 and reflect on whether you should take a break or keep playing. Have you reached your loss limit or are you close to it? Ask yourself this question.

Once the dealer has given you your twenty chips, stack them in stacks of five chips. This makes it easy to see where you stand at any given moment. When you win more chips continue to stack them in five chip stacks. If you are winning and are starting to get too many stacks in front of you, I have a great solution. Quietly start slipping your bankroll into an out of the way place such as your pocket. Some authors do not recommend you do this, but I do. You will be surprised when you have slowly worked it all into your pocket just how good you feel. At this point you are assured of not losing the current session.

Win and Loss Limits

What should be a good loss limit for a session? Just because you have $200 for the session, you don't have to lose it all. This may be how the old, undisciplined you used to do it, but not any more. The new you is a winner and winners don't lose down to their last chip. John Patrick[20] suggests for a bankroll of $200 to set a 40% loss limit ($80).

Another author, Henry J. Tamburin,[21] states he sets a 25% loss of his session bankroll at one table before he moves on. This doesn't end his session, but he moves on to a possibly more favorable setting. He quits and takes a break if he loses the entire $200, and states, "I head for the pool."

George Pappadopoulos[22] also sets a $200 loss limit for the day. He adds, however, that if you have lost $100 and feel it is not your day, go home. Something else he adds which bears repeating is the casinos are open 24/7, so you will have many chances to win another day.

My opinion is with a $200 bankroll, $100 should be all you need to lose in a session before pausing to consider your options. Take a break, relax, reflect, refresh, and return to win session two.

Setting a win limit is more controversial. Patrick[23] advises his students to quit once they have won twenty per cent of their session bankroll, which would be $40 for the $200 session bankroll. Pappadopoulos[24] uses a 50% figure [$100 in this example]. By setting a low win limit you may increase your percentage of winning sessions. If you have a large loss limit, one losing session may offset two winning ones. You should at least try to equal your loss limit. If you lose $200 in one session but won $50 in three sessions, you can brag about your win rate, but you haven't won.

Other authors feel there shouldn't be a limit, but a system where you keep going and set milestones. The first milestone might be a win of $50, but if you are winning and pass this mark, set a higher milestone. Should you continue to win, great, but should the tide turn and you fall back to the $50 mark, you must stop. Keep on winning and repeat what you did by setting the milestone higher and raising the fall back as well. This is a very appealing system introduced by Tamburin.[25] This system allows you to maximize your winnings at a "hot" table. Just be sure to keep raising your fall back each milestone.

One of the smartest players with whom I have played would simply ask the dealer to hold her spot as she took a break. During the break she went straight to the cashier and cashed in the bulk of her winnings. Once the winnings were in cash, it didn't come out again. From that point on she played with the remainder of the chips she hadn't cashed in. Should her winning ways continue, she would make another trip to the "potty" and cash in more. I'd say she was one smart cookie. Later, I have more about Mrs. "Green."

If you are using the E-Z Bet System, I have some considerations for you. Let's say you have set a 20-unit win goal or $100 with a $5 unit bet. Once you cross ten units won, you should start thinking about playing more conservatively. As you are approaching the fifteen-unit mark, you should set ten units as your milestone to quit should you start losing and going backward. As you approach your twenty units win goal, up the milestone to fifteen units. Once you reach your goal, plus or minus one unit, seriously consider leaving the table.

If you are at a hot table with a cold dealer, and you aren't tired, press on if you desire. Remember to keep raising your milestone and don't get caught up in trying to break the bank, because you can't. This might be a good place to try proportional betting and raise the unit bet by 20%. This would make the $5 unit bet $6, the $10 bet would go to $12, and so on.

Discipline

Discipline involves carrying out the above management rules. Discipline cannot be defined any better than George Pappadopoulos[26] did when he stated, "Discipline… is the unwavering ability to follow the above stated rules to perfection without giving in to emotions." Therefore, you have to set your rules before you sit down. Even before you walk into the casino, have them set. In a way, you are going into battle and you must have a battle plan. Carry out the plan during the session, leave when you have won your limit [or loss limit], and enjoy the spoils of war. Discipline is a characteristic of a winner. Develop discipline and you will become a winner.

Mr. Black

This is a good point to interject a story about loss of control. As a student of the game, I enjoy watching others play. Sometimes I am looking for a table at which to play, so I watch while others play. One day at Harrahs I saw a man color up some greens to black. I believe he had a thousand dollars in blacks and greens. With his last few greens he was going to play just a few more hands.

He was dealt a pair of threes and the dealer had a four up card. He had bet two greens and he decided to split the two 3s, so he put out another two greens. His first card was an eight, so he did the correct play and doubled down on this first of two 3s. He had to break one of his blacks to get the greens for this bet. He received a six on this hand, giving him a seventeen. On the next three he received another three. Again he split these two. Out came another $50 to split. He played out the second three and ended up with a hard 14, but heck, the dealer only had a four up card. His attention turned to the third three. He promptly got another three. This was a six-deck game so this was more possible than with single deck. The action was fast and furious. He pulled out a second black and split the fourth three off. So "Mr. Black" had $250 out on four hands. He finished out the last two hands with low totals for both.

You can guess what happened. The dealer turned over a ten hole card and drew a six, giving a hard total of 20. Mr. Black mumbled some profanity. He then decided to catch up quickly by betting the remaining blacks. He was making the correct basic strategy moves, but the dealer was on fire. The more he lost, the angrier he became and the more he cursed. He bet out the remainder of his blacks, quickly losing the rest of them. In ten minutes he had lost a thousand dollars back to the casino. He stormed out, cursing as he ran.

What are some lessons we can learn from Mr. Black? The *first lesson* is the importance of an adequate bankroll. Mr. Black was adequately bankrolled, at least for $25 chips as the basic unit. But this situation shows how a two-card hand can really turn into four hands. If inadequately bankrolled, one could end up with half of his/her bankroll played at one time. Mr. Black lost five units of $50 each, but after that loss, and before he went crazy, he still had 15 - $50 units left. This is more than enough with which to recover.

The *second lesson* to learn is: do not try to catch up quickly by betting a much larger unit. Blackjack is a game of slow progress. Sometimes it is a game of quick regress, but progress remains slow. If you have a sudden reversal of fortune, don't try to get it back as quickly as it was lost. Just like a coach of a football team, you have a game plan. You do not change game plans just because of a quarterback sack or a lost fumble. The coach will sometimes deviate from the plan, try to throw a bomb to catch up only to see an incompletion and then be forced to do it again. The big difference is the coach has only four downs to make a first down. You, on the other hand, have as many "downs" as needed to get the "yardage" back. Don't feel like you have to get it back in one or two hands.

The *third lesson* is related to the above scenario: control your emotions. The coach above showed a loss of control. The game plan was to give the ball to the tailback who was getting five yards every time he touched the ball. The seven-yard sack could have been mostly recovered if he had faked the bomb and given it to the tailback. He deviated from the game plan. He showed loss of control. Mr. Black lost control and went for the bomb again and again. He deviated from the game plan that had won the thousand dollars in the first place.

If you are emotionally attached to your money you shouldn't be gambling with it in the first place. If you are prone to anger and loss of control, you shouldn't be gambling. Sometimes, no matter how good you are, the cards do not fall for you. It's nobody's fault. It's not yours - you played perfect basic strategy. It's not the dealer's - he/she is just the one who takes the cards from the shoe and places them in front of you. Whether you use my betting strategy or one of the others, you must be prepared to have losing sessions or losing periods within a session. Be in control of your emotions and remember that Blackjack is a cyclical game and the next cycle will be in your favor.

What if you find yourself emotional about an event that occurred? Back off. Cool off. Relax. Regroup. Get back in the game. Remember what happened to Mr. Black. You don't want to get in a vicious cycle like Mr. Black. Control yourself. Don't try to catch up quickly. You just might be trying to catch up when the cards are not favorable. Loss of control turned Mr. Black into Mr. Green and, eventually, into Mr. Red Face as he stormed out of the casino.

Mrs. Green

You should try to be keenly aware of the ebb and flow of the game. When a deck cools off, be careful. You may need to ride the storm out or you may need to walk. Mrs. Green was one of the best players I have ever seen at doing just that. Mrs. Green was a very good Blackjack player. She made all the right moves, and won a fair amount of money. While Mr. Black was out of control, Mrs. Green exhibited total control. Mrs. Green was not glued to her seat. When the table cooled off, Mrs. Green would color up and take a break. Sometimes the dealer would save her seat, and sometimes not. Still, every time she came back after her break there was an opening. What she did during her break is very important.

During the break Mrs. Green would go to the cashier and cash out her chips except for just enough to keep her playing. Once she converted her winnings to cash, it might as well been in a bank vault. Mrs. Green was acutely aware of the cyclical nature of the game. Not unlike card counters, when the game cooled, she was aware of it and took her break. By the end of her break, the table had again become favorable or at least neutral, and she was back to playing. You will also become aware of these cycles the more you play. If you are already an experienced player, then you have seen these cycles almost every time you play. Don't be glued to your seat. Feel free to ask the dealer to hold it for you and get up and take a stretch break, go to the bathroom, or follow Mrs. Green's lead and make a little deposit to your "vault."

You should always be aware of your chip standing. Mrs. Green was. I am always assessing my win/loss status. I am very predictable. I always stack my chips in stacks of five units. When I win above my buy in, I slightly separate the stacks so the buy in is to the left and my winnings are to the right. As the winnings grow, I put the buy in into a stack by itself. This is my untouchable pile. As time passes and more winnings are accumulated, I begin moving winnings to the untouchable pile. Mrs. Green would have taken a break to cash them in, but my technique works for me. Once the table begins to cool off, and I start to dip into my winning stacks to play, I assess if it is time for either a break or time to leave. This is where the discipline comes in. Most casinos are open 24/7, so they will still be there when you are ready to play again. Use your self-control and you will be a winner.

Advice for Picking a Table

So now you've got your bankroll, you've set your loss limits, and you have a strategy to leave a winner. You are determined to leave a winner and have the discipline to leave a winner. You know the basic strategy backward and forward. You know the conservative variations to basic strategy and when to use them. You've picked a betting strategy that works for you and fits your budget. Also, you've read this and other good books on playing Blackjack. You are ready for the casino, right? Yes, but you have to pick a table at which to play.

I have always liked to play at a table with several other players. Playing heads up with a dealer is tough. The play is faster, and you may feel pressure from the dealer. Also, you can't see as many cards as you can when there are several other players. Often when I have a tough call to make I use card observation. I prefer to play at or near third base. This gives me a view of the whole table and I have a little more time to make up my mind how I am going to play. Most decisions are automatic but others may require a little more thought. You can use card observation very easily from third base. You can also keep an up to the minute count from third base.

Do not sit down just yet. Stand where you can see what the dealer is dealing him/herself and what some of the players are receiving. Is the dealer HOT? Or, COLD? Does the dealer bust about three of ten hands? How many stiff hands did the dealer get out of ten hands? How about the players? Are they piling up the chips or are they barely hanging in there? Answer these questions before you sit down. Also ask the dealer and players how the dealer is doing. They will usually be brutally honest. If the advice is positive, take a seat. It's time to play some Blackjack.

My advice is to test the waters before jumping in. Buy in for about ten units and start off conservatively. Flat bet the minimum and see if you've made a good choice. Once you are sure, start the system you have chosen. The table after ten hands should be either neutral or biased toward the player. So you should be up a few units or even with the house. I know this may seem overly cautious, but it is worth it. Now start your progressive system. Give it a good chance to work, but feel free to change to one of the other systems that you have learned. That is why you were presented with them.

If anything changes you can and should drop to a minimum bet for a while. Examples would be changing dealers, a new shoe, players coming in or players leaving. You may be doing great with one dealer or shoe, another dealer comes in or the cards are shuffled, and your cards do a 180.

Finally, if in doubt err on the conservative side. The worst that can happen if you don't double down on a hand is that you miss out on a unit or two. You might need a second draw to prevent a loss. Playing conservatively may end up being the most lucrative Blackjack you ever played. You might be amazed.

Things To Remember

If the table becomes choppy, change to a 2-1-2 system.

Don't be so eager to play that you lose your senses.

Always use a fall back system once you are ahead.

Stick to your pre-set loss limit.

If you are not up after an hour, it's probably not your day.

If you've been ahead and find yourself back to even, it's a bad sign. You should either quit or change tables.

If your system isn't working, nothing will.

If you get a gut feeling you should go, leave.

If someone is frustrating you with his or her play, leave.

The longer you're in the store, the more you are going to spend. This goes for grocery stores and casinos.

Sometimes a dealer (or shoe) is going to kick your rear.

It's OK to leave when your rear is getting kicked.

You won't always win. The systems in this book are good, but not infallible. Keep a loss in perspective.

Check the chair before you sit down. Look for glue. If there is any glue in the seat, don't sit down. You don't want to be glued to a chair. Probably a loser sat there before you.

Should you lose seven in a row, or about 11 units using the conservative losing sequence, take a break, change tables or both.

Recognize when the cards aren't falling your way. Sitting out a hand may totally change the flow of cards.

Always be aware that no matter how good your system is doing, it can turn on a dime.

Lastly, no matter how good a system is, it can be beaten. But, you don't have to be.

Making E-Z Bet work For You

First, **know E-Z Basic Strategy**. Know it forwards and backwards. Know it inside and out. Know it up and down. You need to know the correct move to make. You also need to know when to play more conservatively. Instances will come along where you want to play it safer. At the same time, have confidence that the strategy is the most correct way to play a hand and, in the long run, will prove to be right. You will be amazed at how many people play Blackjack without having ever looked at a basic strategy. These are the people who split tens, hit hard eighteens and stand on stiffs when the dealer shows a ten. These people are either ignorant, stupid, or both. So, learn E-Z Basic Strategy first. It is fundamental.

Second, **have an adequate bankroll**. I subscribe to the session bankroll of 40 times your unit bet. Don't cut this too close. You might be the next one to get four threes. If you over bet your bankroll you could end up like Mr. Black . You come into a game in progress. You do all you can to pick a good table, but the dealer turns into Attila the Hun and you drop twenty units before you turn around. This seldom happens, but it can. Be adequately bankrolled and you can weather any storm. Rest assured, you will seldom need all forty units, but you never know when you will.

Third, **pick a progressive betting strategy**. I hope you will use mine, but whichever you choose, practice, practice, and practice some more. You will need more practice with the basic strategy than with the betting sequence. You have to keep up with where you are in the sequence. This is simple with the simple sequences, but the intermediate and advanced systems can be more challenging. For example, using Simple System 1 all you have to know is the current bet and the outcome of the hand to determine what the next bet will be. On the other hand, with an intermediate system, you have to know which sequence you are on. You may find an identical bet on both the winning and losing sequences. You may even find an identical bet within the same sequence.

You can use any number of ways to keep up with where you are: chips, fingers, or neurons. I prefer not to use neurons since I have a limited number of them, so I use chips. The way I play E-Z Bet is to prepare the next bet of the series while playing. I know which sequence I am in and now I know what the next bet should be. If I lose, the L-2 bet is one unit, so I adjust. If I win, I simply slide out the prepared bet and pull the other chips. In a losing series I know the next bet if I win is to be a two-unit bet. If I lose, I simply slide out the prepared bet. This works well for me, but you can come up with any system as long as you don't get confused.

Fourth, **set your limits**. Which limits should you set? Start with the most important one: the session loss limit. The session loss limit can be all or part of your session bankroll. You may want to be conservative and set a 20-unit loss limit. If this is the case, buy in for only 20 units. If you set a 40 unit loss limit, still buy in for only 20 units. Keep the other 20 units in cash. Should you lose the first 20 units, take a short break and assess the situation. Do you want to continue to play at this table, or, is it time to look around? Have the cards turned? Should you simply wait out this shoe? Answer these questions before resuming. This might be the right time for lunch or dinner. It may be time for a bathroom break, a cup of coffee, or a short walk.

Other limits should be considered. Do you have a time limit? Do you have a meeting to attend or a plane to catch? Don't get caught up in the game and miss something important. I guarantee the table will be there when you return.

Should you set a win limit? Probably not. I do not leave a winning table. I like to see stacks of chips in front of me. If you aren't limited by time, stay until the tide turns. Be keenly aware of your chip status. As you play more you will develop a sixth sense about the ebb and flow of the game. Often your fellow players will be very vocal when the tide turns for the house. However, you may be winning when they are losing, so the best barometer is your chip stack. Set your fall-back point and should you fall back to it, pick up your chips. It's time to go.

Yield not to temptation. One last area to discuss regarding playing E-Z Bet is whether you can drink and enjoy yourself and still take the casino for some cash. I generally do not drink alcoholic beverages while playing. If I do have a drink, I keep it low key, alternating with sodas or coffee. With E-Z Bet you can relax more than a card counter can, but you still have to play a strong game. You don't want to lose your inhibitions and blow a winning session. So my advice is to spread out your drinks over the session. Should you find yourself feeling like you may have exceeded your safe limit, STOP! Let it wear off before resuming play. The casino would love to see you become uninhibited. You may find the waitress bringing you drinks before you order them. That is a bad sign. Don't let them make you into a loser with cheap booze.

When you get close to the end of your session, order your favorite brand and savor it as you walk toward the cashier.

I hope the information in this book will serve you well. I have full confidence that it will. Keep in mind you probably will not get rich playing Blackjack. Most people who go out to a casino aren't looking to get rich anyway. They just want to enjoy themselves. They want to have fun gaming, enjoy a show, have a great meal, and not lose their shirt in the process. Use the E-Z Strategy and E-Z Bet and you will have the casino paying for your great gaming holiday.

Glossary

Note: some terms have dual meaning.

Action: The total amount of money wagered during a Blackjack session. If you play 60 hands in an hour with an average bet of $10, you would have $600 in action.

Anchor: 1) Synonymous with third base. The position to the dealer's far right. The anchor is the last player to play prior to the dealer. Third base is the most desirable seat because you are last to play so you have plenty of time to look over the cards just dealt and make your playing decisions. 2) It keeps the boat from drifting.

Barr, Barring: To be barred is to be refused permission to play. Often, a person caught counting cards or suspected of doing so will be barred from play.

Basic Strategy: The mathematically correct way to play a Blackjack hand. (Billions of hands were played to create the basic strategy charts. The earliest ones were created to play single deck Blackjack, but as casinos have changed to multiple decks, the charts have been recalculated to be optimum for multiple decks.)

Bet: The amount of money or chips played on a hand. Also known as a Wager.

Betting Spot: The circle on the Blackjack table in front of the player where the bet is placed.

Black: $100 chips.

Blackjack: If the first two cards dealt to a player are an Ace and Ten-value card, he has a blackjack. Blackjack pays 3:2 meaning every unit is paid off with one and a half units. A blackjack cannot be beaten, but may be tied or pushed if the dealer has blackjack also.

Break: Also known as bust. The player breaks when the hand total exceeds 21. This is an automatic loss. Should the dealer bust, all players who have not previously busted or settled will automatically win.

Burn/Burn Card: To burn a card is to take the top card after shuffling and place it in the discard pile.

Bust: See Break. Also see Pamela, Dolly...

Cage: This is where the cashier is located for making financial transactions such as cashing out.

Card Counting: A method of keeping track of cards to possibly get an advantage over the casino. Usually high cards are assigned a negative one and low cards are assigned a plus one, or some variation of this. The goal is to increase the bet when ten cards are in excess in the remaining cards to be dealt. Conversely, when tens are in less than their normal concentration the bet is reduced, usually to the table minimum.

Card Observation: A technique of scanning the table looking for clues to the value of the dealer hole card and possible upcoming cards.

Cashier: Located in the cage, the cashier can assist you with financial transactions. Just don't ask for a loan.

Cashing out: To convert your chips to cash at the cage.

Chips: Colored coins of different denominations used to place bets at the table. Red chips are $5; green chips are $25; black chips are $100. The casino logo is usually printed on them. Goes well with dip.

Choppy: 1) Play when there are alternating wins and losses. Some betting systems can counter a choppy table. 2) The water when I go fishing.

Color Up: To exchange lower denomination chips for a higher denomination "color", such as red for green or green for black. This keeps from depleting the dealer's tray.

Comp: Short for complimentary. This can be in the form of a free meal, show tickets, or more, depending on the action you are giving the casino.

Continuous-shuffling machine: A type of shuffling machine that holds four decks of cards and acts as both a shuffling machine and shoe. After cards are played, they are placed into the back of the C. S. M. and are immediately shuffled in with the remaining cards.

Counter: One who counts cards.

Countermeasures: Techniques used by the casino to foil the counters. The countermeasures may include use of multiple decks, rule changes, shuffling up, poor penetration and continuous-shuffling machines. They might also beat the heck out of you.

Cut: To divide the deck(s) using a plastic card (the cut card) into two parts. The dealer then reverses their position, top portion to the bottom. This assures the players of a fair shuffle.

Dealer: 1) The dealer deals the cards, conducts play, makes payoffs, and collects the lost wagers. 2) A supplier of illegal pharmaceuticals.

Dealing Box: Also known as a shoe, the dealing box holds the cards in multiple deck games prior to dealing. The shoe allows one card to be dealt at a time.

Deck: A set of 52 playing cards that may be used for Blackjack, poker and other games. Multiple decks are used routinely to play Blackjack, each with 52 cards. Six decks contain 312 cards.

Double Down: To double down, or just double, a player places a second bet on his/her hand and receives only one more card. The bet may be made for less than the original bet. This move is very advantageous to the player, allowing a larger bet to be placed during a favorable situation.

Draw: To request another card from the dealer. Also known as hit.

Even Money: To ask for even money is to request payoff equal to the wager when the player has blackjack and the dealer has an Ace up. It is the equivalent of taking insurance.

Eye in the Sky: The sky is the ceiling above the gaming tables. Both mirrors and cameras overlook the play, looking for cheaters, counters, and cheating dealers. Everyone is suspect. Disputes may be settled using the video recording.

Face Card: Cards that have a "face" on them: King, Queen and Jack. Also known as paint.

First Base/First Baseman: First base is the position to the dealer's far left. This person is first to be dealt cards and also first to act on his/her cards.

Flat Bet: A flat bet is the same bet every hand. The flat bettor will usually lose in the long run due to the house advantage.

Floorman: Middle Management in the pit. The floorman supervises several tables, ranking in the middle between dealers and the pit boss.

Front Money: Money, or credit, required by the casino to qualify a player for a free trip. Included might be food, transportation, and lodging.

Green: 1) A $25 chip. 2) Also a very small patch of grass that my golf balls avoid.

Hand: Refers to either the original two cards a player receives, or the final total of your cards.

Hard Hand/Hard Total: A hand that has a firm value. This could be a hand of any value which doesn't contain an Ace, or, where the Ace(s) count as one.

Head Up/Head On/ Head to Head: Playing against the dealer alone, one on one, mano y mano.

High Roller: A big bettor. Not synonymous with a good player.

Hit: To receive a card from the dealer. The term "hit me" is the request for another card, not to be slapped around.

Hole Card: The dealer's down card. It remains unseen until the dealer finishes with the player's hands and the dealer plays his/her hand.

House: Another term for the casino.

House Advantage: The long-term casino advantage on any game.

House Rules: The rules of play established by the casino. Examples of rules that may vary from house to house are whether the dealer stands on all 17s, hits soft 17, availability of surrender, double down on any two cards, 10 and 11 only, and so forth.

Insurance: A side bet on whether the dealer has a blackjack when showing an Ace. The player bets one half his/her wager on whether the dealer has blackjack. If the dealer has one, the player is paid twice the insurance bet. If the dealer doesn't have blackjack, the bet is lost. Then play resumes. Generally, insurance is a bad bet, favoring the casino.

Junket: 1) A short gambling trip, often with a group.
2) What I should do with my pickup.

Marker: A draw against a credit line established with the casino.

Martingale: Also known as doubling up, the martingale system is a negative progression betting system. The player doubles the wager after every loss until a win occurs. Long losing streaks and table limits make this an unusable system.

Money Management: A collective term for how one bets, limits losses, holds on to winnings, and bankrolls gambling sessions. Also it includes techniques on how you manage to get money from your wife to go to the casino.

Multiple Deck: A term for Blackjack played with more than one deck of cards. This could be 2, 4, 6, or 8 decks. Better than not playing with a full deck

Natural: See Blackjack.

Nickels: A term for five-dollar chips.

Northern Nevada/Northern Nevada Rules: The area of Reno/Tahoe and other towns in northern Nevada. This area is known for restrictive rules on doubling down and great skiing.

Odds: The probability of something occurring. Odds of winning a hand, receiving a certain card, or getting a blackjack are examples.

Paint: 1) Another term for face cards. 2) Needed on my pickup.

Pat Hand: A hand totaling 17-21. To stand pat is to stand on a pat hand.

Penetration: The depth into the deck(s) to which the dealer deals. Usually penetration is expressed in percent, such as 75% penetration.

Pit: A circular arrangement of gaming tables, where players are outside the circle and only casino personnel may enter the inside.

Pit Boss: The casino manager responsible for the pit. He/she supervises floormen and dealers.

Pitch Game: Games played with 1 or 2 decks where the dealer deals or pitches the cards to the players. The cards are dealt face down and the player can hold the cards. In contrast, shoe games are dealt face up and the player may not touch the cards.

Press Bet: To increase ones bet after winning. This would be considered a positive progression system of betting.

Progression: A technique of increasing ones bets after winning or losing. Positive progressions increase the bet while winning. Negative progressions increase the bet after losses.

Push: A tie. No money changes hands. See also shove.

Quarters: A term for $25 chips.

Reds: 1) A term for $5 chips or nickels. 2) A team from Cincinnati.

Re-shuffle Card: Card used to indicate a point in the deck(s) at which to shuffle the cards again. Usually the cut card is placed in the deck as the re-shuffle card. The position represents how far the deck(s) will be penetrated. Also called a shuffle marker.

Round: A complete hand for the players and the dealer, from the first card dealt to the last.

Sequence: A betting sequence is a set way of varying ones bets. The 2-1-2 system has an exact sequence of bets to follow.

Series: 1) A series is a group of the same outcomes. A series of losses is a group of losses in a row. A group of wins in a row is a winning series. 2) What the Yankees usually win. 3) What the Red Sox finally won again.

Session: A period of play at the tables is a session. A session may be short or long, and there may be several sessions per casino visit. A session is usually followed by a rest break.

Session Bankroll: The amount of money you take to the tables for a session. A recommended session bankroll is 40 times your minimum bet, or 40 units if your unit is also your minimum bet.

Shoe: A box or container that holds the cards for play with four or more decks.

Shuffle/Shuffling Up: To mix the cards well prior to play. Types of shuffling are riffling, stripping, boxing and washing.

Shuffling Machine: A device which holds a number of decks of cards, usually six, and shuffles the decks while a second set of decks are being played with.

Silver: $1 chips used at lower minimum tables and for tips.

Single Deck Game: The original Blackjack game played with one standard deck of 52 cards.

Soft Hand/Soft Total: A hand containing an Ace counted as an 11.

Split/Splitting Pairs: When dealt a pair of cards of equal value the player may divide the two and, after placing another wager, play them as two hands. Generally Aces receive only one card after splitting, while others may be hit as many times as necessary.

Stand: To stand firm; to decide not to take additional cards.

Stiff Card: A dealer up card between 2 and 6.

Stiff Hand: A player hand with a value between 12 and 16.

Surrender: 1) To choose not to play a hand, and receive one half of the wager back. There are two types of surrender, early and late. The most common is late surrender, which happens after the dealer checks his/her hole card for blackjack. 2) What America will never do.

Ten/Ten Card: Any card that has a value of ten: the 10s, Kings, Queens and Jacks. The number that comes after nine.

Ten Poor: 1) A situation when an excess of ten cards have been played in proportion to the non-tens. 2) Me and nine of my buddies.

Ten Rich: 1) A situation when an excess of non-ten cards have been played in proportion to the tens. 2) Bill Gates and nine of his buddies.

Ten Tracking: Watching the number of ten cards that have been played to assist in playing or betting decisions. This can be done in a number of ways such as counting cards, card observation, or estimation.

Third Base/Baseman: The position to the dealers far right. This player is the last to act before the dealer acts on his/her hand.

Tip/Toke: A token of your appreciation given to, or bet for, the dealer. Dealers make most of their living from tips so if one is extra nice, please tip. If they are rude, forget it.

Tray: The container in front of the dealer where the house's chips are stored.

Unit: The lowest bet you will make. A unit can be any multiple of a standard casino chip. For example, a $5 unit would be one red, while a $10 unit would be two reds. Two Reds would equal one Cardinal.
Up Card: The dealer's exposed card.

Vig/Vigorish: A term for the house percentage in a casino game.

Wager: See Bet.

Whale: An extremely high roller. This is the player who gets all the comps and perks the casino has to offer.

Index

A

Advanced Systems 55
Advanced System #1 55, 78, 84
Advanced System #2 56, 80, 84

B

Bankroll 95, 100
Basic Strategy 3, 4, 17
Bet 9
Betting Circle 10
Black, Mr. 98
Blackjack 9
Braun, Julian 4
Break 11
Buildup 56
Bust 11

C

Card Counting 2, 87, 88
Card Observation 33, 35, 40-42, 56
Cardoza, Avery 94
Casino Verite 59
Chips 10, 95
Choppy 49, 51, 54
Continuous Shuffling Machines 8

D

Dahl, Donald 49
Discipline 98
Double Down 13
    Hard 27
    Soft 27
Draw 11

E

Eye in the Sky 8
E-Z Basic Strategy 20-24, 106
E-Z Bet 58, 81, 84
E-Z Count 89

F

Fibonacci Sequence 57
First Base 10
Flat Betting 43, 64, 83, 84

G

Green, Mrs. 97, 101-102

H

Hard Doubling Down 24, 27
Hard Hand 11, 26
Harvey, Richard 47, 55-56, 88
Hit 8

I

Insurance 9, 42
Intermediate Systems 50
    Intermediate System #1 50, 76, 84
    Intermediate System #2 51, 77, 84
    Intermediate System #3 52, 78, 84

L

Loss Limit 96

M

Martingale 46, 65
Money Management 2, 5, 93, 94

N

Natural 9

P

Pairs 14, 29-30
Pair Splitting 14, 24, 29, 30
Pappadopoulos, George 52, 94, 96, 98
Patterson, Jerry 56-57
Pat Hand 11
Patrick Basic Strategy 20
Patrick, John 20, 51, 94, 96, 97
Pit Boss 8
Popik, David 20, 50
Problem Hands 33
Progression/Progressive Betting 45
Proportional Betting 57, 98
Push 9

R

Reno 18, 65
Running Count 89

S

Sequence 45
Series 48-52, 57, 61-68, 72, 73, 77,79,81,107
Session 57, 63, 95-98, 101, 107-109
Session Bankroll 96, 106
Shoe 7, 8
Simple Systems 47
Simple System #1 47, 73, 84
   Simple System #2 48, 74, 84
   Simple System #3 48, 74, 84
   Simple System #4 49, 75, 84
   Simple System #5 49, 75, 84
Single Deck 1, 4, 8, 9, 18-22, 35, 39, 59,87,91,92,99
Soft Hand 12
Soft Doubling Down 12, 24, 27-28
Split 14
Stand 9
Stiff 12, 15
Surrender 9, 41

T

Table, Blackjack 7
Takedown 56
Tamburin, Henry 48, 49, 57, 96, 97
Third Base 10, 33, 34, 35, 88, 103
Thorp Basic Strategy 4, 18, 20, 28
Thorp, Edward O. 4, 5, 18, 20-22, 24, 39, 63, 91
True, Count 89

U

Unit 20, 33, 35, 36 43, 45, 47-57, 60-67, 73-79

W

Wager 9
Win Limit 96

References

1) Thorp, Edward O: *Beat The Dealer.* Vintage Books, New York, 1962.
2) Thorp, Edward O: *Beat The Dealer.* Vintage Books, New York, 1962.
3) Popik, David S: *Winning Blackjack Without Counting Cards.* Citadel Press, New York, 1984.
4) Patrick, John: *So You Wanna Be A Gambler! Blackjack.* Metuchen, New Jersey, 1983.
5) Thorp, Edward O: *Beat The Dealer.* Vintage Books, New York, 1962.
6) Harvey, Richard: *Blackjack The SMART Way.* Mystic Ridge Books, Albuquerque, 1999.
7) Tamburin, Henry: *Blackjack Take The Money and Run.* Research Services Unlimited, Greensboro, 1994.
8) Dahl, Donald: *Progression Blackjack.* Kensington Publishing Corp., New York, 1993.
9) Popik, David S: *Winning Blackjack Without Counting Cards.* Citadel Press, New York, 1984.
10) Patrick, John: *So You Wanna Be A Gambler! Blackjack.* Metuchen, New Jersey, 1983.
11) Pappadopoulos, George: *Blackjack's Hidden Secrets-Win Without Counting.* Lynwood, New Jersey, 1999.
12) Harvey, Richard: *Blackjack The SMART Way.* Mystic Ridge Books, Albuquerque, 1999.
13) Patterson, Jerry L: *Blackjack: A Winner's Handbook.* The Berkley Publishing Group, New York, 2001.
14) Tamburin, Henry: *Blackjack Take The Money and Run.* Research Services Unlimited, Greensboro, 1994.
15) Harvey, Richard: *Blackjack The SMART Way.* Mystic Ridge Books, Albuquerque, 1999.
16) Thorp, Edward O: *Beat The Dealer.* Vintage Books, New York, 1962.
17) Patrick, John: *So You Wanna Be A Gambler! Blackjack.* Metuchen, New Jersey, 1983.

18) Pappadopoulos, George: *Blackjack's Hidden Secrets-Win Without Counting.* Lynwood, New Jersey, 1999.

19) Cardoza, Avery: *Essential Blackjack Wisdom.* Cardoza Publishing, New York, 2002.

20) Patrick, John: *So You Wanna Be A Gambler! Blackjack.* Metuchen, New Jersey, 1983.

21) Tamburin, Henry: *Blackjack Take The Money and Run.* Research Services Unlimited, Greensboro, 1994.

22) Pappadopoulos, George: *Blackjack's Hidden Secrets-Win Without Counting.* Lynwood, New Jersey, 1999.

23) Patrick, John: *So You Wanna Be A Gambler! Blackjack.* Metuchen, New Jersey, 1983.

24) Pappadopoulos, George: *Blackjack's Hidden Secrets-Win Without Counting.* Lynwood, New Jersey, 1999.

25) Tamburin, Henry: *Blackjack Take The Money and Run.* Research Services Unlimited, Greensboro, 1994.

26) Pappadopoulos, George: *Blackjack's Hidden Secrets-Win Without Counting.* Lynwood, New Jersey, 1999.

About the Author

Billy Joe Garner lives in a small town in middle America. He has a wife, Linda Jo, and two children, one dog, two cats, three horses, and a donkey. He drives a pickup and a tractor. You might say he's a Country Joe.

Billy Joe has a Masters degree in Nurse Anesthesia from The University of Texas Health Science Center-Houston, and his Bachelors degree from The University of Texas Medical Branch-Galveston.

Billy Joe has lived in small towns across America. He grew up in Mississippi, not far from where Elvis was born. Other towns where Billy Joe has lived include Atlanta, GA; Houston, TX; Los Angeles, CA; and Reno, NV. It was in Reno where Billy Joe fell in love with Blackjack and conceived some of the original ideas for this book. Currently he plays in ST. Louis, MO, and Tunica, MS because his pickup can make it that far.